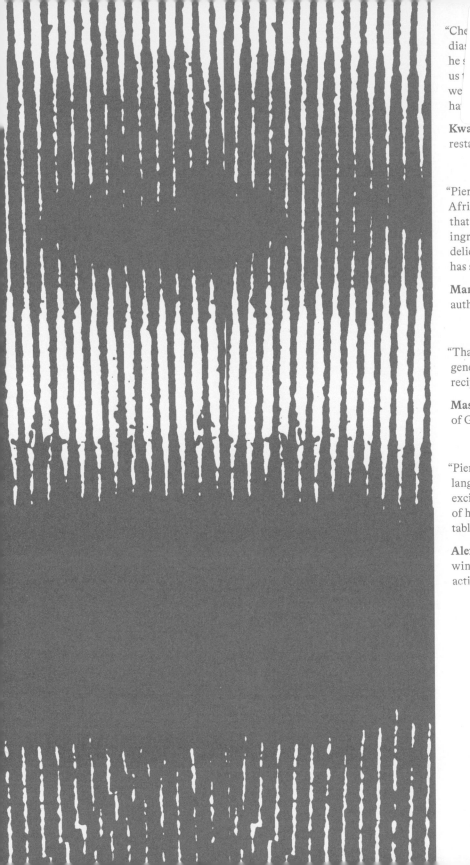

CW00548094

"Che...
dias...
he s...
us f...
we...
ha...

Kwame Onwuachi, ...
restaurateur

"Pierre shows off the vibrancy of West
African cuisine in an approachable way
that demystifies West African spices,
ingredients, and techniques to make
delicious wholesome food. This book
has so much heart."

Maneet Chauhan, chef, restaurateur,
author, and TV personality

"Thank you, Pierre, for sharing your
generous storytelling and wonderful
recipes with the world."

Mashama Bailey, chef and cofounder
of Grey Spaces

"Pierre Thiam has created a culinary
language and narrative, translating his
exciting cultural history into a potpourri
of heritage and flavors for the modern
table. This book is a gift to the world."

Alexander Smalls, James Beard Award–
winning chef, restaurateur, author,
activist, and owner of Alkebulan, Dubai

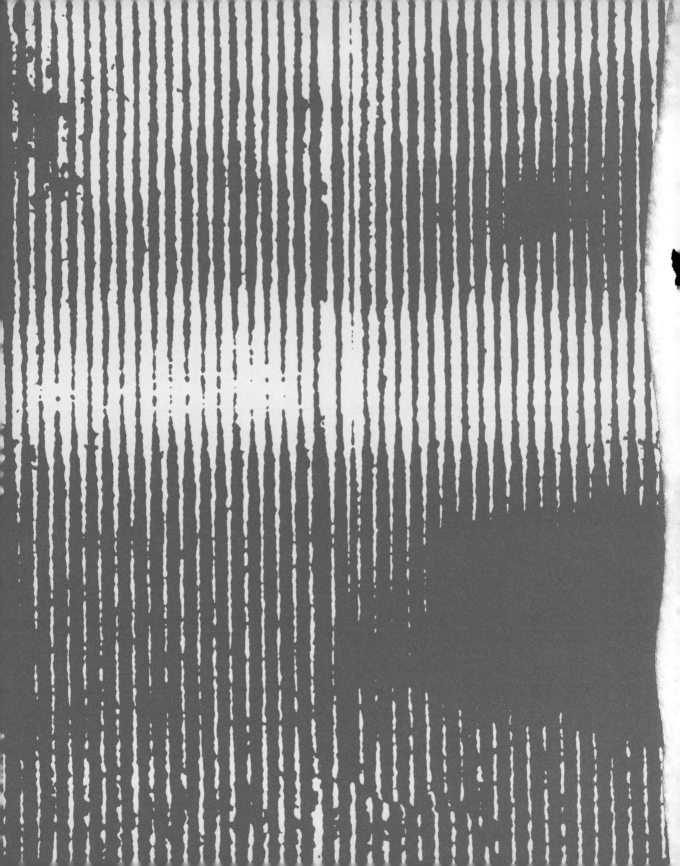

SIMPLY WEST AFRICAN

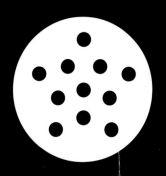

EASY, JOYFUL RECIPES

FOR EVERY KITCHEN

PIERRE THIAM

with
Lisa Katayama

Photographs by
Evan Sung

Clarkson Potter/Publishers
New York

SIMPLY WEST AFRICAN

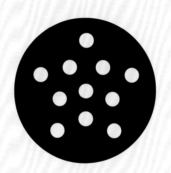

EASY, JOYFUL RECIPES FOR EVERY KITCHEN

Copyright © 2023 by Pierre Thiam
Photograph copyright © 2023 by Evan Sung
All rights reserved.

Published in the United States by Clarkson Potter/
Publishers, an imprint of Random House, a division
of Penguin Random House LLC, New York.
clarksonpotter.com

CLARKSON POTTER is a trademark and
POTTER with colophon is a registered trademark
of Penguin Random House LLC.

Library of Congress Cataloging-in-Publication Data
Names: Thiam, Pierre, author.
Title: Simply West African / Pierre Thiam ; with
Lisa Katayama ; photographs by Evan Sung.
Description: New York : Clarkson Potter/Publishers,
[2023] | Includes index. |
Identifiers: LCCN 2023007098 (print) | LCCN
2023007099 (ebook) | ISBN 9780593578025 (hardcover) |
ISBN 9780593578032 (ebook)
Subjects: LCSH: Cooking, West African. | Cooking—
Africa, West. | Quick and asy cooking. | LCGFT:
Cookbooks. | Recipes.
Classification: LCC TX725.W47 T48 2023 (print) |
LCC TX725.W47 (ebook) | DDC 641.5966—dc23/
eng/20230317
LC record available at https://lccn.loc.gov/2023007098
LC ebook record available at https://lccn.loc.
GOV/2023007099
ISBN: 978-0-593-57802-5
Ebook ISBN: 978-0-593-57803-2

Printed in China

Photographer: Evan Sung
Food Stylist: Pierre Thiam
Prop Stylist: Leila Nichols
Editor: Jennifer Sit
Editorial Assistant: Bianca Cruz
Design: Rush Jackson Studio
Production Editor: Terry Deal and Natalie Blachere
Production Manager: Philip Leung
Compositor: Merri Ann Morrell
Copy Editor: Deborah Weiss Geline
Indexer: Elizabeth Parson
Marketer: Monica Stanton
Publicist: Kristin Casemore

10 9 8 7 6 5 4 3 2 1

First Edition

FOR NAIA

SAUCES

THE NOT-SO-SECRET SAUCE TO WEST AFRICAN CUISINE

SNACKS

NOSTALGIA-INDUCING TREATS

MEAT

SIMPLE COMFORT FOODS

SEAFOOD

JOYFUL FEASTS FROM THE SEA

VEGETABLES

NOT JUST A SIDE HUSTLE

GRAINS & BEANS

NO WEST AFRICAN MEAL IS COMPLETE WITHOUT THEM

INTRODUCTION

People used to talk about Africa as if it were a faraway place that's hard to get to and different in every possible way from the rest of the world. Not anymore. It's time to release these outdated stereotypes and misconceptions, because Africa is everywhere. It's in our past, present, and future. Africa is at the root of human history. It is the place where humans first discovered fire, a necessary first step for cooking and civilization. Its rhythms are embedded in popular music, its textures and colors in contemporary art. Most important, Africa is home to the youngest population in the world: 70 percent of our people are under the age of thirty. Africa is the future! Every day, our youth create culture and design innovative solutions to the world's biggest challenges. Africa connects us more deeply with ourselves, with one another, and with our planet. Trace almost anything that humans touch backward or forward in history, and it will take you to Africa.

AFRICA IS EVERYWHERE.

IT'S IN OUR PAST, PRESENT, AND OUR FUTURE.

This book was written so that you, too, can connect to Africa, in the most delightful and intimate way I can possibly imagine—through the food you cook and eat at home. I grew up in Senegal, a breathtaking coastal country in West Africa. A lot of the food we love to eat, no matter where we are in the world, connects back to the region of my motherland. Traditional West African cuisine is among the healthiest in the world, with its lean meats, abundant vegetables, leafy greens, legumes, and hearty beans and grains prepared in ways that honor the integrity of the source ingredient while bringing out a mélange of flavor possibilities along the way.

I have now lived in the United States for more than half my life and work as a chef, entrepreneur, and activist centering my activities around West African and West African–inspired food. With this book, I will show you how you can bring the joy of West African culture into your life with great-tasting recipes that are easy enough to make at home and impressive enough to serve to royalty. You'll get a glimpse into my world, where Africa meets America, where complex flavor palates meet simple cooking techniques, where family, community, and diaspora all come together in unity and harmony.

My previous cookbooks focused on representing West African food as it exists in the motherland. This time, I bring you a lineup of recipes that shows you how easily West African cooking can be incorporated into your weekly repertoire, without compromising authenticity and deliciousness. Each of these dishes was designed so that it can be cooked in any kitchen with easy-to-source ingredients to create a mouthwatering, one-of-a-kind meal. From the sun-kissed coconut-limey palate of Brazil to the Spanish paella brought to Europe by the Moors to the sultry one-pot gumbos and stews in the American South, West African influences are truly everywhere. Even if you've never had West African food before, you'll quickly experience how familiar its flavors are. Evolution and adaptation are a core part of our culture and cuisine, and you'll see this reflected in the vast variety of tastes and preparations represented in these unique and still very characteristic West African recipes.

The recipes in this book serve as reminders of how much all humans have in common with one another. I don't mean this in a Pollyanna-ish way. There are many very serious inequities and challenges that face our world, especially when it comes to racial, economic, and social issues. In this moment in global history, our collective moral conscience is being challenged to elevate itself. We are being reminded to honor and appreciate one another's cultures and identities in new and evolved ways. (Appreciation is different from appropriation, which is when members of a majority group adopt cultural elements of a minority group in a disrespectful, exploitative, or stereotypical manner.)

My life's purpose is to bring West African–inspired food to every kitchen, regardless of where in the world that kitchen might be. Through the food of my home region, I want to showcase the beauty of a culture that's centered around community.

Where I come from, food is more than just a collection of ingredients in a bowl. The West African cook is a griot of sorts, a storyteller who connects us to our past, our present, our future—and to our environment. Every recipe is a story that transcends time and space, having been passed on by our ancestors to their children and their children and so on, and now to you, through this book. I'm so excited to welcome you to this world! When you cook the food from this book, you become part of the story, a key member of the community of people who cook and enjoy contemporary West African food at home. You will expand your horizons, tap into the innermost essence of your joy, and fill your kitchen and dining areas with some of the richest, most delectable smells, sights, sounds, and tastes you've experienced.

BRINGING WEST AFRICAN VALUES AND FOOD TO YOUR HOME CAN FUNDAMENTALLY CHANGE HOW YOU ENGAGE WITH THE WORLD, IN THE MOST BEAUTIFUL AND POSITIVE OF WAYS. HERE'S TO FINDING YOUR AUTHENTIC JOY—AND SHARING IT GENEROUSLY WITH THOSE YOU LOVE.

AN ODE
TO
TERANGA

THERE'S A WORD IN WOLOF, THE SYRUPY MOTHER TONGUE OF MY NATIVE SENEGAL IN WEST AFRICA, THAT PERFECTLY DESCRIBES THE SPIRIT OF OUR FOOD CULTURE. THAT WORD IS *TERANGA*.

Teranga is when someone sees you coming their way and greets you with the warmest welcome, hands you a much-needed beverage or a piping hot plate of whatever they were having for lunch, then thanks you for stopping by as you go back on your way, belly and heart full. There's no English word that translates perfectly, but if I had to create a dictionary definition, it might look something like this:

Teranga
[*teh-RAN-gah*]
(noun):

1. a quality of generosity, love, warm welcoming, and abundance

2. a character trait often expressed via a radically inclusive, perpetual cycle of joy

Having teranga means you're vibing to the continuous drumbeat of a living, breathing, sharing community. It's one of the features of West African culture that is at once nonnegotiable and irresistible—a necessary comfort in a sometimes lonely world. Teranga is a Senegalese concept, but it's also ubiquitous in the African diaspora. Everywhere African people go, we bring the spirit of teranga with us.

Teranga is a powerful unifying force, one that shows us how to find joy in even the most difficult situations. Teranga played a role in bringing hope and community to the millions of West Africans who arrived in America unwillingly through the Middle Passage. And it continues to play a role today in allowing people to tap into an uncompromising strength and happiness in even the most challenging situations. Teranga teaches us how to treat one another with love and respect, no matter what else might be going on inside or outside of ourselves. When things get hard or complicated in my life, I always remind myself of the generosity that teranga embodies.

I wrote this book with my wife and my best friend, Lisa. I met her in Tanzania, where I gave a TED Talk in 2017. Apparently, it was a really good talk, because she remembered me the next morning when we sat across from each other on a shuttle bus to a breakfast meeting we'd both been invited to, and we had a great conversation. Lisa is a writer and activist, among many other things, and she knows what's going on in my head sometimes better than I do. Even in our first conversation, she instantly grasped my mission and purpose, and articulated it back to me in such a way that I knew I had to keep her in my life somehow. By the time the idea for this book project came up a few years later, she and I were raising a small child together.

Lisa grew up in Japan, a culture that also has a long and well-known ritual of teranga. Omotenashi, the Japanese version of teranga, looks and feels different from the West African version, but the underlying values—generosity, hospitality, and deep care—are quite similar. Perhaps as a result of this, we both love hosting friends and neighbors at home, sharing everything from books to snacks to toys to clothes with each other, and finding different ways to pepper our home life with appreciation.

By reading this book, I hope you will learn how to incorporate the spirit of teranga—an essential ingredient to a life of generosity and abundance—into your daily life, just as we do.

FROM MY WORLD TO YOURS

Why did I become a chef?

The answer is pretty simple.

I love food.

I love everything that food represents. Food is such a beautiful way to experience the diversity of the world and to explore the connections between cultures. Have you ever bit into something from a culinary tradition other than your own and found it to be delightfully reminiscent of a flavor your taste buds already know? Or traveled to a faraway place where people use tools and techniques that look just like the ones your grandmother used? Food transcends borders, and the legacies of our ancestors reside within every dish, between every bite.

I love feeding people. It gives me a sense of deep satisfaction that I would never be able to adequately express through words. Words are not my love language. Food is. I'm one of those chefs who also cooks at home. My favorite moment of every day is around 6 p.m., when I get to announce "Dinner is ready!" and my wife, Lisa, and daughter, Naia, come clambering down the stairs from whatever playtime they were engaged in to indulge in my latest profession of love, presented on fragrant, steaming platters. I love how Naia's eyes get wide with excitement when she sees her little ocean-blue plate filled with all the colorful foods she's about to try. I love watching Lisa reach for seconds, sating her hunger after a long day of working and parenting. Everything begins and ends with food at the table. Mine is a love-centered approach to cooking. When you start with love, everything else follows.

I love the kitchen. The kitchen is my safe place. When I'm in the kitchen, whatever stress I was carrying with me goes up in flames—literally!—and is quickly replaced with the infinite possibilities of culinary alchemy and a presence of mind. For me, being in the kitchen is a spiritual experience akin to sitting in quiet meditation or communicating with the ancestors. Every moment is an opportunity for me to express my creativity and gratitude through food. I keep my kitchen clean and organized. It's my place of work, and I like it to feel understated and spacious, like a modern art gallery with lots of room for breathing and reflection. I am a strong believer in the power of simplicity when it comes to the kitchen. The world is complicated enough. Our kitchens don't have to be.

I love the act of dining with others. Nothing compares with the magical feeling that is created when people of all walks of life come together to tell stories over shared meals, or when hungry hands reach from all directions toward an appetizer plate at the start of dinner, unified in a shared experience of joyful anticipation. I believe that the primary role of food is to nurture communities and the people in them, and to remind them of what's most important—health, happiness, and the essence of life that is brought to us through the act of preparing and consuming meals with others.

I love eating. I hate being hungry. I am, at the core, a practical person. Early on in my life, I figured out that one of the best ways to make sure I would never be hungry was to always be near an active working kitchen. As a kid, I used to hang around my mom—because I loved her, of course, but also because being around her meant I got to liberally sample the things she was preparing to serve to her five kids for dinner. I grew up sandwiched between two older brothers and a younger sister and brother, all of whom were always running around and very hungry. In retrospect, I realize that the gravitational pull I felt to be near food at all times may have been a signal of my calling to become a chef, and not just the immediacy of my hunger. Years later, when I found myself in America and in need of a job, I once again found myself drawn to the allure of the kitchen. This is how I first entered the restaurant world.

SOHO,
NEW YORK CITY
1990s

It was a vegetarian dish that convinced me that West African food needed to have a seat at the global culinary table. It was the early '90s, and I was a recent transplant from Senegal, working as a young cook at Boom, one of the hottest restaurants in SoHo at the time. New York City was supposed to be a short pit stop on my way to the Midwest for university, but while staying in a boardinghouse in a yet-to-be-gentrified, seedy Times Square, my life savings was stolen out of my suitcase, and I got stuck. To recoup the funds and try to get back on track, I got a job as a busboy at Garvin's, a small American restaurant in the West Village, where I spent my days shuttling dirty plates to the kitchen, refilling glasses of ice water, and wiping down greasy tables between customers. From there I moved to the back of the house, where I worked my way up the kitchen ladder from dishwashing to peeling onions and chopping carrots to assembling appetizers and salads. I was always the hardest-working, most dedicated guy in the back of the house, and I was steadily promoted one small step at a time. In those first few years in New York City, I worked at some great establishments, learning alongside many talented and wonderful cooks. The kitchen became my life. Somewhere along the way, I gave up on college and committed myself to staying in the restaurant business. After all, I was in the food capital of the world. There was so much more to explore and learn, even without a formal education.

When Boom opened, I was working at a little spot nearby called Jean Claude that served French bistro classics to an upscale Manhattan crowd. Everybody was talking about the new "global ethnic" restaurant started by a tall, young, and handsome California surfer–looking guy named Geoffrey Murray. Murray had traveled extensively to places like Indonesia, Thailand, Vietnam, and Malaysia and had designed a menu that was a beautiful reflection of the food of those regions and beyond. Even though New York City was already overflowing with dine-out options, this type of fusion cuisine was still novel and definitely very popular. Among the early clientele were Madonna, who ate there regularly; Prince, who once jumped on stage to play a song with our house band; and Bob Dylan, who famously hosted a party with guests like David Bowie, Iman, and Allen Ginsberg. The waiting list for a table reservation was months long. There was no question in any New York foodie's mind at the time: Boom was the place to see and be seen.

During one of my lunch breaks from my gig at Jean Claude, I decided to take a short walk around the corner to Spring Street, where Boom was located. I was curious to get a whiff of the exciting new flavors and energy of the place, to see for myself what all the buzz was about. Even though I probably couldn't get a table there, I wanted to read the menu and soak in the scene, if only from outside. I was milling around the front of the establishment in my chef whites when I bumped into Chef Murray, who had just stepped out for his own break. Feeling shy but determined, I introduced myself and told him that I wanted to learn from him, expecting at best that he would hand me an application and send me on my way. Instead, he looked at me dressed in my chef's jacket and said, "Well, you seem ready to work. Follow me into the kitchen!"

At Boom, my culinary adventures quickly turned from a slow and steady simmer to a rapid, rolling boil. This place was on fire! And I'm not just talking about the crowd, the energy, and the ambiance. For me, the excitement was all in the flavors of the food we served. They were bold, spicy, fruity, fermented . . . a brand-new expression of a type of diversity and eccentricity that reminded me, oddly enough, of the food from my motherland. In fact, these vibrant qualities took me straight down memory lane to my Vietnamese godfather's amazing kitchen back home in Senegal. Vietnam and Senegal have a shared colonial past. Many Senegalese soldiers fought in the Indochina War for France's army, and my uncle Jean arrived in Senegal as a teenager with his mom and sister in the 1950s. When I was growing up, Jean Gomis was the only man I ever saw cooking. In most Senegalese homes, you saw only women in the kitchen, but walk into Uncle Jean's home at any given moment and you'd see a slim Asian man chopping freshly grown cilantro, Thai basil, lemongrass, and Japanese eggplants from his backyard garden, then effortlessly whipping up incredible-tasting dishes from Southeast Asia while singing some traditional Vietnamese tunes. My palate has always been multicultural, thanks to the influences of Uncle Jean. I can still taste his rich, tangy pho broth.

I WAS CONVINCED I HAD TO DO MORE TO SHARE THESE TRADITIONS WITH THE WORLD.

IF PEOPLE WERE ECSTATIC OVER MAFÉ, JUST IMAGINE HOW MUCH THEY WOULD LOVE YASSA, EFO RIRO, AND NDAMBE!

Working at Boom opened up my palate of experiences and brought lots of pieces together. I was witnessing new ways of blending flavors. Murray would do surprising things like cook otak otak (a traditional Indonesian fermented fish paste wrapped in banana leaves) over an open grill, or apply a classic Vietnamese five-spice treatment to a grilled quail. He made an unforgettably refreshing tatsoi with carrot ginger salad dressing and a beautiful flat rice noodle with coconut and prawns. Before Boom, you had to go to a hole-in-the-wall, tiny restaurant to get this type of food, but Boom brought it to the mainstream, presenting these multiethnic meals in beautiful clay bowls reminiscent of the cultures they came from, without cheapening or appropriating them. Dining at Boom was a true feast for the senses—distinct fragrances floating through a sultry space filled with impeccably dressed patrons eating artistic plates of food. Meanwhile, as the restaurant gained traction with New York's in crowd, I continued to make my way up the kitchen ladder, going from cold apps garde-manger to manning the grill to mixing the sauces to even trying my hand as a pastry chef. I was excited to go to work every day. I was living in the most happening city in the world, doing a job that I loved. New York had just elected its first Black mayor. Everything felt possible.

Murray took notice of my enthusiasm and thirst for learning. He became a mentor and a friend. We would meander through nearby Chinatown in search of unique ingredients, some that smelled and tasted strikingly similar to the ones from my mom's kitchen. The Southeast Asian fish sauce tasted like the funky dried salted fish called guedj in Senegal. The Malaysian shrimp paste smelled like the fermented locust bean known as dawadawa, or netetou. Whenever I went shopping with Chef Murray, I felt like a kid in a toy store. He shared his knowledge and experiences, and I occasionally told him stories of the food I had eaten in West Africa.

One day, Chef Murray asked me if I wanted to try out one of the dishes from Senegal for a special menu he was planning to launch. I often prepared Senegalese dishes from memory at staff meals, and he wanted me to introduce one on the main stage. Wow, what an honor! I thought (even though I was playing it cool on the outside). Here I am, this immigrant kid from Dakar, and I get to try my very own recipe on the elite gourmands of New York City. So I took a small risk and whipped up a vegan rendition of the classic Senegalese mafé. The rich, beautiful, irresistibly nutty mafé is one of the mother sauces of African cuisine, traditionally prepared with chicken or beef, but I made mine with colorful, warming vegetables like carrots, cassava, and cabbage. In America, we often think of veggies as sides, but in traditional West African cuisine, vegetables play an equally important center-stage role as meats. In my own little way, I wanted to show this audience what my food was all about.

My root vegetable mafé hit the menu, and on the second day that it was being served, a food critic happened to be dining at the restaurant. She ordered the mafé and loved it so much that she wrote an article about it in her newspaper, the *New York Post*. Thanks to this unanticipated press, the dish ended up staying on the menu for longer than intended. As I watched the hippest cats in the world devour and delight over this nutritious, plant-based dish devised by my ancestors centuries ago, I was convinced I had to do more to share these traditions with the world. If people were ecstatic over mafé, just imagine how much they would love yassa, efo riro, and ndambe!

I had found my calling.

CALIFORNIA
2023

Many years have passed since then, but my purpose has remained the same. I have operated three restaurants in New York and published three cookbooks. I have traveled around the world to more than two dozen countries to introduce modern West African cuisine to the world, and to speak about the importance of eating climate-friendly foods for the future. I've cooked for celebrities, presidents, kings, and youth communities. I've worked in numerous kitchens ranging from multimillion-dollar private estates in upper Manhattan to bare-bones industrial kitchens in places that very few people get to visit. I've collaborated with NGOs like the United Nations World Food Programme and the International Fund for Agricultural Development and corporations like Kellogg's and Unilever—always advocating for a more diverse, sustainable diet for the good of our planet and its inhabitants. In the past five years, I started two key ventures that bring me to today: an African food company called Yólélé, and a fine-casual restaurant chain called Teranga.

With everything I'd done up until then, I saw how powerful sharing recipes, stories, and special dining experiences was in spreading the word about the traditions and values of West African food to even more people. But a critical missing piece was the availability of ethically sourced, reliable quality African ingredients in everyday stores. Yólélé was created with the mission to promote African food culture to the global market and support small farmers from West Africa whose livelihoods were being negatively impacted by food imports and mass production of common crops like corn, wheat, rice, and soy. My cofounder, Phil Teverow, and I partner with farmers' collectives in West Africa that produce underutilized crops like fonio, millet, and sorghum, which are then packaged and distributed for a global audience. We asked Paula Scher, superstar graphic designer from the world-renowned design firm Pentagram, to build a recognizable, unabashedly African brand identity. Today, you can find Yólélé's fonio pilafs, chips, spice blends, and flours in Whole Foods and Target stores across America. On the supply side, we are building a processing mill in Mali and a distribution hub in Senegal. And there's much more to come.

Teranga, my latest brick-and-mortar restaurant, was born out of a desire to create a physical space where New Yorkers could convene to eat delicious, home-made West African food in a modern, unintimidating, casual setting. For our flagship Harlem location, we partnered with the Africa Center, a nonprofit institution dedicated to engaging with and promoting Africa, and brought in cool creatives like Nigerian American Victor Ekpuk and Ethiopian-born Ezra Wube to adorn our walls with their symbolic modern art. The resulting ambiance is one where anybody who loves Africa will feel right at home while still experiencing the prestige of being on Manhattan's world-class Museum Mile, across from Central Park and just minutes from the hustle and bustle of Harlem's finest establishments. Walk into Teranga Harlem at any given moment and you'll be welcomed by the irresistible scent of home-cooked, ready-to-serve West African classic eats, the sounds of kickass Afrobeats, shelves lined with Afrocentric literature and cookbooks, and communal tables filled with patrons from all walks of life tossing generous amounts of spices and sauces onto their plates. Teranga has been listed repeatedly among the best restaurants in New York, and we also distribute packaged meals throughout the United States through meal subscription services like CookUnity.

The journey is continuous, and it's always a delight to find myself collaborating with great chefs and establishments across the world, whether that's back home in Senegal with the Pullman Dakar Teranga Hotel or right down the street from where we live today with the inimitable Alice Waters at Chez Panisse in Berkeley, California.

✦✦✦✦✦✦

Sometimes people label me as an African chef, but this identification isn't entirely accurate. The food in this cookbook is a unique blend of African ingredients with flavors, methods, and inspiration from literally every corner of the world. My cuisine is both unapologetically West African and globally relatable. This indelible link between where I come from and where I live today is a core part of my belief about how we can all be best equipped to navigate this increasingly interconnected earth. I always encourage young chefs to revisit their roots, dig up the culinary traditions that ground them, and cultivate their knowledge of the tastes and techniques of their origin cultures before they venture out to build their own signature styles. When you develop your craft in this way, you make it your own, without forgetting where you come from. You develop a presence of mind and spirit that will nourish and support you on your journey through life. It's my hope that this book's exploration of West African cuisine can build a new connection between my world and yours.

I know that saying this in a cookbook is a little funny, but writing down recipes is an imperfect science. Cooking is more than just following a set of instructions. Recipes are useful guides, but they are not the ultimate source of truth. This is because there are always tiny variations in size, flavor, and texture of an ingredient that a home cook must tune into. A yellow onion grown in a hot dry climate like Senegal will taste different than one grown in a greenhouse in the Colorado winter. While these differences may sound like a challenge, this is actually the key to making you a better cook, because it invites you to use all of your senses when you're in the kitchen.

The recipes in the book are solid, reliable guidelines that will make sure you create a great dish. But, if you feel called to add a dash of fish sauce or to stew your beans a bit longer for a softer touch, by all means go for it! Think of this as an opportunity to allow your intuition to express itself safely. The combination of these recipes and your intuition is what will make your dish uniquely yours.

I call this approach conscious cooking because it requires all the senses. Too often, we go through our days on autopilot, without tapping into the presence within us. Cooking can be your cue to connect to your senses and feelings. This is therapeutic and inspiring! When you make conscious cooking a practice, you will eventually get to a place where all your senses are awakened the moment you enter the kitchen. You'll start to pick up on the nonverbal but deeply informative language of food. When you cook ingredients consciously, you'll start to hear how they are stringing together sentences and paragraphs of the most beautiful, edible prose. Practicing conscious cooking helps you make deeper and more visceral connections to the food you eat every day.

As you prepare the recipes in this book, always keep in mind this intuitive approach to cooking. Using this strategy will guide you beyond the recipe steps and make your cooking a personal, almost spiritual experience. This is a practice that will develop over time, one that I feel is so important to anyone who spends time in a kitchen, recreationally or otherwise. It is, after all, the creation of food—one thing in life that we cannot live without.

THE PRINCIPLES OF CONSCIOUS COOKING

1. AWAKEN YOUR INTUITION

This is probably one of the most important beliefs I inherited from my mom, my aunties, and others in my family who shared their recipes with me. Every single sight, sound, ingredient, tool, and motion contributes to the final outcome of your creation. Intuition, in a culinary sense, is that little voice in your head that says things like "Pssst! Maybe you need a little more salt!" or "Hmm . . . what if you sneak in a few drops of lemon to enhance the acidity of this delightful concoction?" Cooking with intuition is a multisensory act. Every aspect of an ingredient—the texture of a grain of fonio, the color of a ripe plantain, the sound of the oil crackling in the pan—serves as a potential clue as to what to do next. Knowing how to follow a recipe is a strong indicator of success—and it helps, of course, to have a good knife to chop with—but my most precious and irreplaceable kitchen tool is my intuition.

2. PRACTICE PRESENCE

Cooking is my meditation, my therapy. It brings things into focus in an otherwise chaotic-feeling world. When I'm in the kitchen, nothing else matters. I am present but not tense, taking in the sights, the smells, the flavors, the textures, the sounds. When you combine presence with the art of cooking, every sense takes part in the creation process. When you shop at the market, you are connecting with the ingredients as they communicate their readiness to be used or consumed. When you look at the food as it cooks, you are taking in the changing chemistry of the ingredients. When you listen, you listen for the sounds of readiness. And when you sit down to eat at the table, you actually taste the food.

3. CULTIVATE JOY

You must find as much joy in cooking as you do in eating. Take the time to make the kitchen a fun, joyous place for *you*. Clean it, organize it, have a glass of water or wine, or play some background music that relaxes you. Put on some comfy clothes! For me, nothing beats cooking breakfast in my pj's while Naia happily eats yogurt and berries next to me. What does your inner music sound like? Mine sounds like a jazz trumpet, so I often listen to Miles Davis or Dizzy Gillespie while I'm prepping my space. When I'm in the zone, even cleaning the dishes becomes enjoyable.

4. INGREDIENTS MATTER

The selection of ingredients is a very important component of what makes a truly great cook. There is no better way to assess the quality of your ingredients than by looking, touching, smelling, and even, if possible, tasting them at the market. If you connect with them, they will respond to you and give you what you need. The fish tells you it's fresh by the firmness of its flesh, the brightness of its eyes and gills, the salty sea-breeze aroma that lingers. Every piece of fruit or vegetable has its own personality depending on how it was grown, how much sun and water it received, the type of soil it grew in, and how long it was left to mature before harvest. Your specific eggplant or okra may need a little extra something that only your intuition can tell you. It's also important to try to buy ingredients in season to sustain and nurture the earth, instead of depleting it of its precious resources via overfarming, over-irrigation, and overuse of chemical fertilizers and pesticides.

5. SHARE THE LOVE GENEROUSLY

The best part of cooking for me is watching the people I cook for eat my food. I love seeing the pleasure on their faces as they devour my latest creations. Cooking is a great way to nourish your loved ones, but it's also a radical act of love and kindness to self. When I cook, I know that I'm making something that's good for me and good for the planet and good for the people who are going to eat it. It's in moments like this that I realize that I have the best job in the world. I feel so blessed to be able to call cooking my profession because there is so much fulfillment that comes from it. Cooking is a powerful act that brings healing and happiness. One of the foundations of the West African culinary experience is that food is shared, and for this I recommend that you always make a little extra: Making food in the spirit of teranga means always having more for the unexpected guest. If they don't show up, the dish always tastes better the next day anyway.

SETTING UP YOUR WEST AFRICAN KITCHEN TOOL KIT

You don't need a fancy kitchen or a super decked-out set of tools to start cooking West African food. When you go to West Africa, you'll see a range of tools being used across the region, regardless of whether you're in bustling cities like Lagos or Abidjan or the most remote villages accessible only after a day of road travel. Conscious cooking requires us to care for our things, regardless of how new or old, fancy or basic they are. I am delighted to share with you the kitchen tools I swear by. Whether I'm in my home kitchen in Northern California or cooking off-site, I always make sure I have access to the following items. Whenever possible, I like to use tools that are closer to nature—made of materials like wood, fibers, and stone. Doing that feels better and more aligned with my beliefs, and it allows me to cook food more lovingly; that ultimately makes the food taste better, too.

8-INCH CHEF'S KNIFE

We do a lot of chopping and cutting in West African kitchens, so you will need at least one good multipurpose chef's knife. I use a Japanese chef's knife at home. I also always have a paring knife and a cleaver handy. Having a complete knife set is great, but one good 8-inch chef's knife will go a long way. Keep a steel or stone knife sharpener handy, too, unless you have frequent access to a knife-sharpening service.

CAST-IRON COOKING POT

Often with African cooking, a good stew or one-pot dish ends up cooking in a single vessel for a long period of time. For this, a cast-iron pot can be incredibly useful. It is reliably durable and well suited to conducting heat at high temperatures. I use my cast-iron pot to fry, simmer, braise, and oven roast many of my creations. At home I have a Le Creuset 9-quart enameled cast-iron Dutch oven.

SLOTTED SPOON

We do a lot of one-pot cooking in West Africa, but sometimes the various ingredients in that pot have different cooking times. Slotted spoons are incredibly useful for scooping vegetables out of stews and sauces selectively without messing with the stock or other ingredients. They're also great for blanching different vegetables in the same pot of water (see page 189), without having to waste water or reboil it. I use a 12-inch stainless-steel slotted spoon at home.

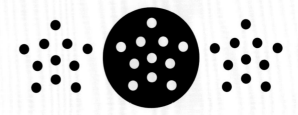

MORTAR AND PESTLE

In Senegal, mortars and pestles are our food processors, used to make spice mixes and ingredient blends that are at the heart of our cuisine. In traditional African kitchens, they're carved out of tree trunks, which are often bulky and not very convenient in an apartment kitchen. A mortar and a pestle give you a more wholesome, refined grind that retains flavor and essence much better than an electric spice grinder. At home, I have a small tabletop mortar and pestle made out of granite stone that I use to blend fresh garlic, parsley, and other fresh ingredients, as when I make Garlicky Parsley Rof (page 49) or Nokos Seasoning (page 33). I also have a ceramic bowl with ridges that I use with a wooden stick for mixing dry spice blends like kankankan (see page 32). If you don't have a mortar and pestle, you can use a regular spice grinder.

COUSCOUSSIER OR STEAMER

West Africans love to steam our grains and vegetables. This simple, effective process helps retain nutrition and textures that complement our stews and sauces perfectly. A commonly used tool in West and North Africa is the couscoussier, a two-part food steamer that's shaped a little bit like a snowman. You can easily search online for one wherever you live. Alternatively, you can make your own steamer at home by putting a smaller colander inside a bigger pot with a lid. The colander should be able to sit comfortably in the pot, with enough space between the bottom of the colander and the base of the pot so that water doesn't touch the grains or vegetables.

WHISK

You'll want to have a good whisk to mix cooked vegetables with sauces directly in the pot. Traditionally, we use a tool called a blending broomstick—a handheld, broomlike tool made of thin palm fiber straws tied together on one end by a fabric handle. But a standard-size stainless-steel whisk will do just fine, too.

TONGS

I use tongs to do a lot of different things in my kitchen: to salvage freshly fried pof pofs (page 82) from hot oil, toss cold salads, and sometimes even to move hot pans in the oven (though I don't recommend this unless you know you're strong and coordinated enough to do so safely). Having one pair of solid, strong 12-inch stainless-steel tongs will allow you to move much more efficiently, especially when you have multiple dishes going at once.

WOODEN SPOONS

Most home cooks in Africa use wooden spoons to stir sauces and stews. It's the best way to avoid the metallic aftertaste that metal spoons can sometimes leave. Plus, they last forever.

SKIMMER

This is not absolutely necessary if you have a slotted spoon, but it's very useful for bigger batches of meats or vegetables that need to be drained of liquids before serving.

BLENDER OR FOOD PROCESSOR

In West African cuisine, there's often a blending stage before or after the cooking phase. I love using my tabletop mortar and pestle, but when I need to make large batches of something, this method is just more efficient. I use a large Cuisinart food processor and a Vitamix blender at home.

RESEALABLE JARS WITH TIGHT-FITTING LIDS

These are perfect for storing the many sauces and condiments that we use in our cooking. I suggest getting a few pint-size jars and a few smaller jam jars for spices and sauces and some masking tape to label them with. At home, we have an entire rack filled with jars where we keep all our dry foods, spices, and grains (a larger version of the jars we use to store leftover sauces in the refrigerator). In addition to its being easy to identify what's in them, it makes a beautiful kitchen display.

OTHER BASICS

If you're stocking your kitchen from scratch, I recommend getting a few stainless-steel bowls, one small and one large stainless-steel pot with lids, at least one nonstick sauté pan, and a wooden cutting board—but honestly, whatever you have in your kitchen now is perfectly okay. If you've ever made pasta at home or fried some eggs, chances are you already have what you need.

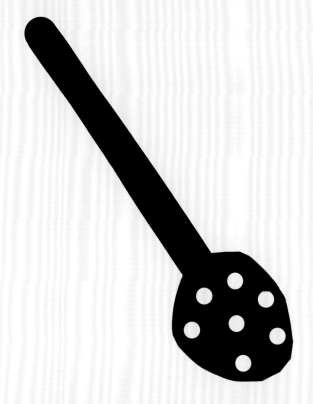

YOUR ESSENTIAL WEST AFRICAN PANTRY

AS YOU BROWSE THROUGH THE RECIPES IN THIS BOOK, YOU MIGHT BE ASKING YOURSELF QUESTIONS LIKE "WHAT EXACTLY IS FONIO?" OR "WHERE IN THE WORLD DO I GET DAWADAWA?"

THE FOLLOWING SECTION GUIDES YOU THROUGH HOW TO SET UP YOUR BASIC WEST AFRICAN PANTRY.

In West Africa, ingredients like baobab, moringa, amaranth, coconut, and fonio—many of which are now being marketed as "superfoods"—have been a core part of our everyday diet for centuries. Our people, and indigenous peoples all over the world, have traditionally used every part of these incredibly resilient, amazing plants for their livelihood. This is a waste-free, efficient way to utilize Mother Earth's precious bounty—an important reminder to look around at our natural environment and make use of what surrounds us, instead of limiting our diet to overmanufactured monoculture crops. It is a great act of love for both our planet and ourselves to replace our dependence on corn, wheat, rice, and soy with other nutritious and delicious ingredients. It also helps us be part of the solution, not the problem, to food security—making sure that there is enough food on the planet to feed eight billion-plus people.

Sourcing the items listed here and mixing a couple basic spices from this section will give you a head start, a solid foundation that sets you up to be a successful West African home chef. Think of it as a gentle packing list for the journey you're about to embark on.

THE MUST-HAVES

FONIO

WHAT IS IT

Fonio is a small, seedlike, gluten-free super grain packed with protein, vitamins, and minerals. It's good for your nervous system and great for your heart. When cooked, it's fluffy and nutty and as versatile as plain white rice or bread—but so much quicker to prepare, healthier, and more delicious! My previous cookbook, *The Fonio Cookbook*, was dedicated entirely to recipes using this grain. The magic of fonio doesn't end with its health benefits; growing it is also great for the planet. Fonio requires very little water to grow and thrives in regenerative agricultural systems, meaning it nurtures the earth it is grown in rather than destroying it. This is incredibly important right now as the world faces unprecedented biodiversity loss because of climate change and the overexploitation of resources like fish and wildlife. There is a recipe for basic fonio on page 215 and a few dishes throughout the book that use it as a base.

WHERE TO FIND IT

You can buy sustainably sourced, responsibly harvested fonio at Yolele.com.

IF YOU DON'T HAVE IT

Couscous has a similar texture, but it contains gluten; rice or quinoa will keep your meal gluten-free.

SUSTAINABLY SOURCED RED PALM OIL

WHAT IS IT

Also known as red gold, red palm oil has a unique vermillion tint and full-bodied floral accents that enhance any dish cooked with it. It is a nutritional powerhouse rich in vitamins, beta-carotene, and antioxidants, and it's also extremely efficient to produce, requiring much less land to grow than other types of oil-producing vegetables. Palm oil has been the source of some controversy because other parts of the plant, like the colorless oil from its kernel, are important to other industries that include cosmetics and processed foods, and the overuse of this type of palm oil has caused mass deforestation and the destruction of biodiverse ecosystems around the world. This is why it's important to use sustainably sourced red palm oil at all times.

WHERE TO FIND IT

Any natural grocery store will have some options. I use the Nutiva brand at home and large jugs imported directly from the motherland.

PEANUT BUTTER

WHAT IS IT

Unlike in the United States, where it is mostly used as a spread with jelly on a sandwich, in West African cuisine, we use peanut butter as a thickener and flavor agent for our stews and sauces.

TOMATO PASTE

WHAT IS IT

Very simply, tomato paste is concentrated tomato that's been reduced to a paste. It usually comes in a jar, can, or tube. In West Africa, we add it to sauces and stews that require a deeper savory element without compromising the natural flavors of other ingredients.

FISH SAUCE

WHAT IS IT

When it comes to fermentation, I have a simple philosophy: the funkier, the better. Fermented flavors are a key pillar of African cuisine, but when traditional ingredients are not readily available, Asian fish sauce comes to the rescue. Fish sauce is made by putting fresh fish in a barrel and covering them with huge amounts of sea salt until they are cured, then pouring water over everything. After some steeping and filtering, this eventually becomes what we know as fish sauce. A little fish sauce goes a long way in bringing out the umami—a Japanese word used to describe the deep, rich, savory flavor profile yielded by some fermented foods—in your West African sauces when you don't have dried fish or dawadawa (see page 34).

WHERE TO FIND IT

Any Asian market or natural grocery store will have a solid fish sauce. I use the Viêt Hu'o'ng Three Crabs and Red Boat brands at home.

COCONUT

WHAT IS IT

Coconuts are endlessly versatile and can survive almost anything. In West Africa, we use coconut milk for cooking stews, coconut water for drinking, coconut meat for eating or making flour for bread, coconut oil for making butter, coconut sap for making sugar, and coconut leaves for keeping food wrapped up or as roofing materials in homes. If you love coconut, you have to try my Triple Coconut Waakye Rice and Beans (page 218), which uses coconut milk, coconut oil, and shredded coconut.

KANKANKAN

WHAT IS IT

Kankankan is a solid, multipurpose spice blend that you'll want to store next to your garam masala, Italian spice blend, za'atar, and the rest of your global spice collection. It hails from the Hausa tribe from northern Nigeria and can be used in a marinade or as a dry dip. Also called yaji in other parts of West Africa, it's a key spice in making suya, a grilled meat preparation found all over the region. (I have a yakitori-style chicken suya recipe on page 103.)

WHERE TO FIND IT

You can buy premixed kankankan online at Talimasafricanmarket.com, Afritibi.com, or at a West African grocery store.

IF YOU CAN'T FIND IT

Make your own using the recipe below!

HOMEMADE KANKANKAN

Makes 1 cup

½ cup raw peanut flour or 1 cup roasted
    unsalted peanuts, ground into flour
½ cup yellow masa corn flour, toasted
2 teaspoons fine sea salt
2 teaspoons smoked paprika
1 teaspoon cayenne pepper
1 teaspoon ground ginger
1 teaspoon freshly ground black pepper
½ teaspoon ground nutmeg

In a small bowl, add the peanut flour, corn flour, salt, paprika, cayenne, ginger, pepper, and nutmeg, and stir to combine. Alternatively, pulse the ingredients in a food processor. (Store the spice blend in a resealable jar with a tight-fitting lid for up to 1 month.)

NOKOS

WHAT IS IT
Nokos is a classic Senegalese seasoning that enhances flavor in a way that resembles the moment a magician pulls a rabbit out of a hat at a kid's birthday party. Pure joy and delight! This savory mixture brings new life to pretty much everything, including a dreary day.

WHERE TO FIND IT
Make it yourself! It keeps in the fridge for up to two weeks, so I recommend making a batch and using it to top off any meal that needs a boost. Freeze whatever you don't think you will need within two weeks in an ice cube tray and use for emergency resuscitation to any sauce or stew.

NOKOS SEASONING

Makes 1 cup

2 medium green bell peppers, chopped
4 scallions, sliced
2 garlic cloves
2 bay leaves
1 habanero or Scotch bonnet chili, halved and
    seeded (optional)
2 tablespoons freshly ground black pepper
1 tablespoon grated fresh ginger

In a blender or food processor, combine the bell peppers, scallions, garlic, bay leaves, habanero (if using), black pepper, and ginger, and blend into a soft paste. (Store the seasoning in a resealable jar with a tight-fitting lid in the refrigerator for up to 2 weeks, or divide it in an ice cube tray and freeze for up to 2 months.)

THE NICE-TO-HAVES

DAWADAWA

WHAT IS IT
Dawadawa is a fermented locust bean that's used as a seasoning in many West and Central African countries. Depending on where you are, it might be referred to as iru, netetou, or soumbala. It has a funky smell because of its fermentation, but it is a great ingredient to have on hand, particularly if you want to add a touch of special West African umami to your food. It is also vegan, which makes it a great substitute in recipes that call for fermented fish sauce.

WHERE TO FIND IT
It is available in the form of dehydrated powder or bean balls at West African grocery stores or online at Yolele.com.

IF YOU DON'T HAVE IT
Fish sauce is a fine non-vegan alternative, or use Chinese fermented beans if you live near an Asian market.

GROUND DRIED SHRIMP OR CRAYFISH

WHAT IS IT
Ground dried shrimp and crayfish bring that added burst of umami to some of our most classic recipes, including Gbegiri with Black-Eyed Peas and Red Palm Oil (page 64) and Ghanaian Shito Sauce (page 57). Often, the dried shrimp are sun-dried, and the crayfish, smoked and dried. Because they are both from the shrimp family, they are often used interchangeably. An African crayfish is really a freshwater shrimp—different from the American crayfish, which is similar to a tiny lobster. If you can't find the powder or want to grind your own, you can process whole dried shrimp or dried crayfish to a powder and store it in a resealable jar with a tight-fitting lid at room temperature for 6 to 12 months and almost indefinitely in the freezer.

WHERE TO FIND IT
Any West African grocery store will have some, or you can buy it online.

IF YOU DON'T HAVE IT
The closest substitute is Asian fish sauce.

GHANAIAN
SHITO SAUCE
PAGE 57

MORINGA

WHAT IS IT

Moringa is known for its high protein content and has in recent years been popularized as a superfood in many parts of the world. In Senegal, we nickname it nebedaye ("never die") because of its nutritional and healing properties. Moringa will give you a jolt of wakefulness akin to a small cup of coffee, even though it has no caffeine. If you're a newbie to cooking with this wonderful leaf, try your hand at the delicious Green Moringa Coconut Dip (page 76).

WHERE TO FIND IT

It's available in a powdered form at most health food stores. I like the Kuli Kuli brand because it's ethically sourced and high quality.

IF YOU DON'T HAVE IT

Use spinach.

ATIEKE

WHAT IS IT

Atieke is a couscous made out of fermented cassava root. It's very common in Côte d'Ivoire, but we also love it all over the region. It has the shape of couscous but has a deeper flavor with a mild kick of umami that's quite irresistible.

WHERE TO FIND IT

You can get frozen or dried atieke in West African grocery stores and online.

IF YOU DON'T HAVE IT

A standard store-bought couscous will work, though it will lack the acidity that comes from fermentation.

EGUSI

WHAT IS IT

This beloved seed from the melon family is rich in antioxidants and potassium and has a rich, nutty, creamy texture and flavor that takes me right back to Lagos, Nigeria. We use it in West African cuisine to make many delicious things like Sweet Pepper "Egusi" Sauce (page 60) and Smoked Fish and Rainbow Chard Kontomire Stew (page 147).

WHERE TO FIND IT

You can find it in African grocery stores and online. I like the Nina brand ground egusi.

IF YOU DON'T HAVE IT

Common pumpkin seeds are an acceptable substitute.

HARISSA

WHAT IS IT

Harissa is a traditional Tunisian condiment that adds subtle heat and fun flavor to any dish. It's typically made of red chili, garlic, and coriander. You see it featured in my Crispy Roasted Harissa Brussels Sprouts (page 176), but it's also just a great condiment to have on the side of any dish or as a simple vegetable dip. Its name comes from the Arabic verb *harasa*, which means "to crush."

WHERE TO FIND IT

I like the Dea brand, which comes in a tube and can be found at natural food grocery stores.

IF YOU DON'T HAVE IT

You can get away with using your favorite chili paste instead.

PERFECT THE VIBE

It's really important to get the ambiance right when you're cooking West African food. We are a vibrant, rhythmic, dance-to-the-music-in-your-soul type of culture, and our food reflects that. Physical space is, of course, one environmental factor to consider. Don't worry about how small or large, fancy or basic your home kitchen is. As long as you have a working stove, some pots and pans and bowls, and a little bit of legroom just in case you need to get your dance on, you are perfect exactly where you are. What I really want you to focus on getting right is your mental and emotional landscape. Sometimes, I'm tumbling into dinner prep from a long day of meetings, and my brain feels like a video game screen with multiple ping-pong balls bouncing around like crazy. In times like this, I take these three steps:

1. I spend a few minutes clearing the kitchen of any distractions. Dirty dishes, leftover morsels of food, and other random things that somehow made their way onto the kitchen counter all go away. My work space is clean, and the world is suddenly feeling way more manageable.

2. I wash my hands with a delightfully foamy hand soap, mindfully, as a ritual of sorts to transition into a purer mental state.

3. I ask my smart speaker to play one of my favorite playlists. Within no time at all, my soul is dancing, and all of a sudden I have transformed what might look to the naked eye like an ordinary home kitchen into an aromatic wonderland of delectable West African–inspired creations.

Now that you know a little bit about me and my approach to cooking, it's time to start filling your home with the deliciousness of West African–inspired food.

Here's a simple five-step checklist to make sure you have everything you need:

○

GET YOUR KITCHEN TOOLS.

○

STOCK YOUR PANTRY.

○

REVISIT THE PRINCIPLES OF CONSCIOUS COOKING.

○

PERFECT THE VIBE.

○

TAKE A DEEP BREATH.

SAUCES

THE NOT-SO-SECRET SAUCE
TO WEST AFRICAN CUISINE

THE NOT-SO-SECRET SAUCE TO WEST AFRICAN CUISINE

SAUCES

Sauces are the not-so-secret secret to perfection in West African cuisine. For me, going a week without a saucy meal is like navigating a world without color, music, or fresh air. Yes, sauces really are that essential to my relationship with food! In this life full of constant change and uncertainty, my sauces keep me grounded and rooted. Even the most seemingly mundane dish is instantly amplified when you jazz it up with these euphoria-inducing flavor bombs.

In West African cuisine, sauces are not just a nice-to-have. Sauce is queen. Nobody goes to a restaurant and asks for chicken yassa without yassa sauce or sauce feuille with the sauce on the side. When hungry diners browse a menu, they aren't trying to decide between the chicken or the beef. They are trying to decide if this is a nutty and decadent mafé sauce kind of moment, or if they're in a spicier, anything-is-possible piri-piri type of mood. More than any other cuisine that I have encountered in my decades of cooking, ours relies on sauces as necessary vehicles to the edible journey you're going on with your food. This is important to keep in mind as you start cooking these recipes.

This chapter will ground you in some mainstay staples for your fridge so that you can spread some goodness from the motherland on almost anything you eat. In other words, yes, it is absolutely critical for you, the budding West African home cook, to have homemade Ghanaian Shito Sauce (page 57), Senegalese-inspired Garlicky Parsley Rof (page 49), and Moyo Sauce Goes with Everything (page 56) from Côte d'Ivoire next to your ketchup, mayo, and mustard. These sauces are a great way to keep a steady drumbeat of African flavors in your daily routine and transform just about any dish into a West African–influenced meal. It's the easiest answer to "What's for dinner?" when you are gazing into your fridge, looking for weeknight inspiration. The sauces in this chapter are used throughout the book, so it's important that you are down to try them. But not to worry, my friends: The recipes are quite simple and hard to mess up. In other words, the beginning is a great place to start! Before you know it, you, too, will have a kitchen infused with vibrant, refreshing flavors that bring joy and centeredness to your days.

When you incorporate West African sauces into your diet, you'll experience a full range of emotions through your taste buds. You'll discover how to mix flavors so lively to taste that they'll instantly brighten your day, like those in the Casamance Green Mango Salsa (page 53), and condiments so intense that they might make you cry, like the super-hot Everyday Hot Pepper Kani Sauce (page 59). You'll make the mother sauces of African cuisine, like Mafé Peanut Sauce (page 50) and West African Red Sauce (page 51), without which African food would not be what it is today.

GINGER VINAIGRETTE

MAKES ABOUT ½ CUP

I use a lot of ginger at home. It's great for mood stability and digestion, and it also adds a welcome kick and flavor to everything. Ginger testifies to the fact that we do not need to rely on overprocessed condiments to make something taste great. This classy vinaigrette goes with any salad or cut vegetable. It's also a necessary companion to my Fonio, Kale, and Mango Salad (page 198).

1 garlic clove, finely chopped
1 (1-inch) piece of fresh ginger, peeled and grated
1 tablespoon rice vinegar or fresh lime juice
1 teaspoon honey
1 teaspoon fine sea salt
½ teaspoon freshly ground black pepper
½ cup extra-virgin olive oil

In a medium bowl, combine the garlic, ginger, vinegar, honey, salt, and pepper, and whisk until the salt and pepper dissolve. Slowly stream in the oil, whisking continuously until the oil and vinegar are emulsified. Taste and adjust the seasoning as needed. (Store the vinaigrette in a resealable jar with a tight-fitting lid in the refrigerator for up to 2 weeks.)

SAUCE DAH

MAKES ABOUT 1 CUP

Also known as kouthia in Senegal, sauce dah has a unique foamlike texture and adds a citrusy, herbaceous, spicy kick to any grain-based dish. It can even be used as a dip for crudités or chips. The traditional preparation uses sorrel, a dark and slightly sour herb, but here I use a combination of spinach and okra with a few drops of lemon juice as a substitute. Serve it on the side with classic dishes like Poached Calamari Caldou in Tomato and Lemon Broth (page 150), Rice and Beef Mbahal (page 112), and Thiebou Yapp, the Ultimate Rice Pilaf (page 128), or display it in a glass jar alongside some other staple condiments the way we do at Teranga, my restaurant in New York City. A little goes a long way—two or three tablespoons per person is more than enough.

2 tablespoons finely chopped yellow onion

1 tablespoon fish sauce (optional)

½ teaspoon fine sea salt

½ teaspoon freshly ground black pepper

¼ teaspoon cayenne pepper

4 cups baby spinach

4 medium okra pods, trimmed and thinly sliced

1 tablespoon fresh lemon juice

In a medium saucepan, combine 1 cup of water, the onion, fish sauce (if using), salt, pepper, and cayenne over medium-high heat and bring to a boil. Add the spinach and okra and continue to cook until completely soft and the spinach and okra become a thick mixture, about 7 minutes. Reserving about 2 tablespoons of the cooking liquid, drain the spinach and okra mixture.

In a large bowl, combine the mixture and the reserved cooking liquid. Using a whisk or electric hand mixer, vigorously beat the mixture to incorporate and aerate, until the sauce takes on a foamlike consistency, about 3 minutes. Add the lemon juice and continue whisking until the mixture is airy and begins to turn a light green color, 2 to 3 more minutes. Serve at room temperature on the side of any dish or grain of your liking. (Cool and store the sauce in a resealable jar with a tight-fitting lid in the refrigerator for up to 3 days.)

GINGER
VINAIGRETTE
PAGE 42

WEST AFRICAN
PIRI-PIRI
SAUCE
PAGE 58

GHANAIAN
SHITO SAUCE
PAGE 57

EVERYDAY
HOT PEPPER
KANI SAUCE
PAGE 59

ADVENTURES IN LUNCH: FROM DAKAR TO NEW YORK CITY

When I was growing up in Dakar, lunch was like a national holiday that happened every day. As noon struck, every stiff political suit and restless schoolkid left their daytime hustle and dispersed back into neighborhood streets peppered throughout the sprawling city for their favorite meal of the day.

Some memories fade over time, but I'll never forget this delectable midday reprieve during my formative years. As I walked, nose on full alert, along the short path home from school, the tangy aroma of black-eyed pea and tomato ndambe stew slowly greeted me in one direction as wafts of rich, nutty mafé peanut sauce lured me in another. Trace scents of briny whole fish yassa floated by, but I'd be quickly distracted from them by the familiar scent of my friend Benjo's mama's soupou kanja, okra and seafood stew, now known throughout the American South as gumbo.

On most days, I went to my own house for lunch. As the oddly artsy middle child in a sibling set of five, I was my mom's favorite eater, and besides, nothing compared with her light and flavorful caldou, poached carp on rice, garnished with foamy sorrel leaf and okra relish. But if I detoured midway and ended up at Benjo's table, or made a pit stop at my next-door neighbor Aby's house to feast on her satisfyingly crunchy jollof rice, my mother was okay with that, too. She and I both knew that when you live in a world driven by teranga, there's always room for the unexpected guest at the lunch table. Benjo's mom didn't find me a burden, just like mine didn't mind if I brought a gaggle of voracious teens home with me on caldou day.

Maybe, somewhere deep inside, my mother and I both knew that one day my obsession with food would evolve into a more serious endeavor. Looking back, these childhood foraging adventures were so critical to my love and understanding of cooking.

When I got to America, the new meaning of lunch hit me like a burlap sack loaded with ripe, sweet plantains. Odorless slivers of mystery meat slapped between two wilting slabs of white bread. A hasty bowl of noodles sitting in a bowl with some spinach leaves. A heap of raw greens and nuts with oil and vinegar. This. Is. Lunch? I had to adjust my expectations.

It pained me at first that I couldn't walk into any restaurant (or private home, for that matter) and expect a homemade feast for the senses in the middle of the day. But then, I thought of the saying, Be the change you want to see in the world. And I knew what I needed to do: I needed to offer the world some good old classic African sauces so that their lunches could be more vibrant and delicious with just a dollop or dunk—even if the base is just a slice of bread and some deli meat.

MUSTARD-ONION RELISH

MAKES ABOUT 2 CUPS

The combination of chicken stock, onions, and mustard creates this amazing throw-it-on-anything-to-make-it-fancy condiment that will surely become a staple in your home kitchen. We call this a sauce, but it's more of a condiment. Flavor-wise, it is a close cousin of yassa (page 52), one of the mother sauces of Senegalese cuisine—except without the key acidity of the citrus. In our house, we typically serve it with Thiebou Yapp, the Ultimate Rice Pilaf (page 128), but we also love to put it on otherwise ordinary American classics like a burger or a hot dog.

2 tablespoons extra-virgin olive oil

2 medium yellow onions, thinly sliced

2 garlic cloves, minced

1 cup chicken stock

1 tablespoon Dijon mustard

1 teaspoon fine sea salt

½ teaspoon freshly ground black pepper

¼ cup picholine olives, pitted (optional)

In a medium saucepan, heat the oil over medium-high heat. Add the onions and sauté, stirring occasionally, until they have softened and are beginning to brown, 10 to 15 minutes. Add the garlic and continue cooking, stirring occasionally, until fragrant, 2 more minutes. Add the chicken stock, mustard, salt, pepper, and olives (if using). Reduce the heat to medium and cook, stirring occasionally, until the sauce is reduced and well combined, 5 more minutes. (Cool and store the sauce in a resealable jar with a tight-fitting lid in the refrigerator for up to 1 week.)

GARLICKY PARSLEY ROF

MAKES ABOUT 2 CUPS

I'm so happy to be sharing this recipe with you because (1) everyone (yes, everyone!) needs a delicious, garlicky sauce in their fridge, always, and (2) you get to tell your dinner companions the story of how this chimichurri-like condiment is inspired by the secret ingredient to one of Senegal's most coveted national dishes: thieboudienne. (There is a great thieboudienne recipe in my second cookbook, *Senegal*.) I recommend making rof without stressing about how you are going to use it, because it adds herbaceous vibrancy to whatever it's paired with: steamed vegetables, grilled fish, a simple burger, barbecued everything, and—believe it or not—to life itself. All that from an ingredient list that could not be simpler.

2 cups finely chopped fresh flat-leaf parsley

½ cup extra-virgin olive oil

4 garlic cloves, finely chopped

1 teaspoon fine sea salt

1 teaspoon freshly ground black pepper

1 habanero or Scotch bonnet chili, seeded and finely chopped

Using a mortar and pestle or a blender, combine the parsley, oil, garlic, salt, pepper, and habanero, and grind until they are well blended but the sauce is not entirely smooth, like a fine salsa or chimichurri. (Alternatively, in a medium bowl, combine all the ingredients, using a large wooden spoon, until you get the desired consistency.) (Store the sauce in a resealable jar with a tight-fitting lid in the refrigerator for up to 3 days.)

MAFÉ PEANUT SAUCE

MAKES ABOUT 2 CUPS

Mafé is my go-to sauce whenever I'm feeling a little bit homesick, or lazy, or in need of that warm, fuzzy feeling you get from eating your favorite comfort food. Known as one of the mother sauces of African cuisine, this incredibly versatile preparation can be paired with roast chicken, grilled fish, roasted vegetables, plain rice, or pretty much whatever you want! If you like peanuts, peanut butter, or any kind of peanut-flavored anything, this recipe is definitely for you. While mafé is good fresh off the stove, I also love reheating and eating it the next day, as the sauce tends to improve overnight after the flavors have expanded.

1 tablespoon peanut oil

1 cup chopped yellow onion

1 garlic clove, minced

1 tablespoon tomato paste

2 cups vegetable stock or water

½ cup unsweetened creamy peanut butter

1 bay leaf

1 teaspoon fine sea salt

¼ teaspoon freshly ground black pepper

Pinch of cayenne pepper

In a medium saucepan, heat the oil over medium-high heat. Add the onion and sauté until softened but not browned, about 3 minutes. Reduce the heat to low, then add the garlic and tomato paste and continue cooking, stirring frequently with a wooden spoon to avoid scorching, until the tomato mixture darkens, about 3 minutes. Add the vegetable stock, peanut butter, bay leaf, salt, pepper, and cayenne. Stir well to incorporate the peanut butter into the stock, then allow the mixture to come to a boil. Reduce the heat to medium-low and simmer until the oil begins to rise to the surface and the sauce has a smooth and thick consistency, about 15 more minutes. Serve hot over rice or Simply Fonio (page 215) with the meat or vegetables of your choice. (Cool and store the sauce in a resealable jar with a tight-fitting lid in the refrigerator for up to 1 week.)

WEST AFRICAN RED SAUCE

MAKES ABOUT 4 CUPS

Red sauce is an integral component of West African cuisine, much like tomato sauce is in Italian cuisine. The classic Ghanaian rendition of red sauce often includes shrimp or curry, but I prefer the versatility of this easy vegan version. The single ingredient that gives this sauce its originality is the red palm oil, which has a sweet, floral, earthy flavor that so pleasantly complements the tomato. Red sauce can be used as the base for many dishes, like the regional favorite jollof rice (page 219). In West Africa, we often pair red sauce with fried fish, rice, or roasted vegetables, but you could just as easily use it as a pasta sauce. I often make it in large batches, then divide them into single-serving portions and freeze them—this way, they're always ready to use for a quick improvised meal.

½ cup sustainably sourced red palm oil (see page 31) or vegetable oil

2 cups chopped yellow onion

1 green bell pepper, diced

1 garlic clove, finely chopped

1 (28-ounce) can whole peeled tomatoes

1 teaspoon fresh thyme

1 bay leaf

1 habanero or Scotch bonnet chili, seeded and diced

1 teaspoon fine sea salt

In a medium skillet, heat the oil over medium heat. Add the onions and bell pepper, and sauté, stirring occasionally with a wooden spoon, until soft but not brown, about 5 minutes. Add the garlic and cook until fragrant, about 3 minutes. Add the tomatoes with their juices, thyme, bay leaf, habanero, and salt. Cook until the tomatoes are soft and thickened, mashing up the tomatoes as you go, about 30 minutes. Taste and adjust the seasoning before serving. (Cool and store the sauce in a resealable jar with a tight-fitting lid in the refrigerator for up to 1 week.)

CLASSIC LEMONY YASSA SAUCE

MAKES ABOUT 4 CUPS

There's so much to love about yassa. In this unforgettable briny sauce, the humble onion is transformed into a citrusy caramelized classic of Senegalese cuisine. Mustard or no mustard is the ongoing debate when it comes to yassa sauce. Purists claim that putting mustard in yassa is not the authentic way, but I find both versions equally delicious. I've served yassa on so many occasions, to such a wide range of people, and without fail everybody raves about their experience of eating it. You can use it to top almost anything—grilled chicken, fish, vegetables, and the Black Bean–Cassava Veggie Burger (page 197).

¼ cup peanut or sunflower oil

8 cups sliced yellow onions (½ inch thick), from about 4 medium onions

½ cup fresh lemon juice

4 garlic cloves, minced

1 bay leaf

1 tablespoon Dijon mustard (optional)

½ teaspoon fine sea salt

½ teaspoon freshly ground black pepper

1 habanero or Scotch bonnet chili, left whole

½ cup chicken stock or water

In a large pot, heat the oil over medium-high heat. Add the onions, cover, and allow them to cook, undisturbed, for about 3 minutes; when you remove the lid, the onions should be fragrant and starting to lightly brown. Using a wooden spoon, stir the onions once, then re-cover and cook until the onions are more softened, about 3 more minutes. Add the lemon juice, garlic, bay leaf, mustard (if using), salt, pepper, and habanero. Reduce the heat to medium and continue to cook, with the lid slightly ajar and stirring occasionally to prevent the onions from burning, until they start to caramelize and turn slightly brown, another 15 minutes.

Slowly add the stock while stirring, then raise the heat to high to bring to a boil. Reduce the heat to medium and continue to cook, uncovered, until it reduces down to a thick sauce and the onions are completely soft, about 5 minutes. Remove from the heat, and taste and adjust the seasoning as needed. Discard the bay leaf and remove the habanero (it can be passed around among your guests, to squeeze onto their plates for extra heat). Serve hot over grilled meats or fish with rice or Simply Fonio (page 215). (Cool and store the sauce in a resealable jar with a tight-fitting lid in the refrigerator for up to 1 week.)

CASAMANCE GREEN MANGO SALSA

MAKES ABOUT 2 CUPS

Have you ever spent a summer waiting for a mango to ripen? This recipe pays homage to Casamance, the sleepy seaside town that both my parents hail from, and where I spent many long summer days wishing mangos ripened faster so that I could eat them sooner. This refreshing salsa that will hit your palate like a cool breeze on a hot summer day is inspired by a snack that my siblings and I used to prepare as kids. To select the perfectly unripe mango, look for one that is green to the eye and hard to the touch.

¼ teaspoon cumin seeds

1 cup coarsely grated green mango (using the larger holes of a box grater)

1 cup quartered cherry tomatoes

¼ cup coarsely chopped fresh flat-leaf parsley

¼ cup finely diced red onion

2 tablespoons fresh lime juice

1 garlic clove, minced

½ teaspoon cayenne pepper

½ teaspoon fine sea salt

¼ teaspoon freshly ground black pepper

In a dry skillet, toast the cumin seeds over medium heat until fragrant, about 1 minute. Remove from the pan.

In a medium bowl, combine the cumin, mango, tomatoes, parsley, red onion, lime juice, garlic, cayenne, salt, and pepper, and toss thoroughly. Taste and adjust the seasoning. Serve at room temperature as a topping for sandwiches, grilled meats, or fish. (Store the salsa in a resealable jar with a tight-fitting lid in the refrigerator for up to 3 days.)

THE MOTHER SAUCES OF WEST AFRICAN CUISINE

MAFÉ
PEANUT SAUCE
PAGE 50

WEST AFRICAN
RED SAUCE
PAGE 51

CLASSIC LEMONY
YASSA SAUCE
PAGE 52

SWEET PEPPER
"EGUSI" SAUCE
PAGE 60

If you search "mother sauces" on the Internet, you'll most likely find references to the five classic European sauces: béchamel, hollandaise, velouté, espagnole, and tomato sauce. Here, I want to introduce you to the mother sauces of West African cuisine: mafé, red sauce, and yassa. These are the original mother sauces, from the motherland itself, meaning generation after generation of West Africans have used these as the foundation of the dishes they eat at home with family and cook for guests on all occasions. The flavor palates of many West African dishes are offshoots of these three classic sauces. African mother sauces don't come in mainstream packages (yet), but you can store them for one year in freezer bags or refrigerated in resealable jars with tight-fitting lids for up to two weeks.

MAFÉ: Made from a base of peanut butter, tomatoes, onions, garlic, bay leaves, and water, mafé is a mother sauce that many who come from West Africa or have spent time there have cravings for on a consistent basis because of its signature nuttiness and rich consistency. Mafé is used as the basis for delicious West African classics like Sauce Feuille (page 110) and Root Vegetable Mafé (page 188). Using nuts and seeds to build sauces and stews is seen all across West Africa. Soups and stews made from egusi (melon seeds) are another great example.

RED SAUCE: A classic tomato-based sauce often made with ingredients you won't see in European sauces, like palm oil and dawadawa, smoked fish, or other fermenting agents. It's not so dissimilar in function to the Italian tomato sauce that you can buy in a jar at any bodega or grocery store near you, but it has a smokiness that leaves you with a warm, comforting feeling that you can't forget. You can use red sauce on its own or as a base for things like Kontomire Stew (page 147) and Pumpkin Seed "Egusi" Stew (page 180).

YASSA: A popular onion- and lemon-based West African sauce that hails from southern Senegal. The slow-cooked caramelized onions combine with a generous amount of citrus to create a unique mother sauce that West Africans love to love. Yassa is universally appreciated even by the most culinarily unadventurous. It is also the inspiration for other spin-off sauces in this book, like the Mustard-Onion Relish (page 47), which I use to make my Thiebou Yapp, the Ultimate Rice Pilaf (page 128).

MOYO SAUCE GOES WITH EVERYTHING

MAKES 2¹/₂ CUPS

This refreshing, crunchy, salsalike relish requires no cooking—just some fine chopping and a good mixing spoon will do the trick! It's a great sidekick to anything grilled—fish, chicken, vegetables. Although not a traditional addition, this recipe calls for Dijon mustard. Some contemporary West African cooks (including me) do this to add a sharp and tangy vibrancy to the classic moyo. It's the perfect condiment for anytime a meal needs a little extra something in the flavor department.

1 cup quartered cherry tomatoes

1 cup finely diced green bell pepper

½ cup finely diced red onion

¼ cup extra-virgin olive oil

2 garlic cloves, minced

1 habanero or Scotch bonnet chili, seeded and finely chopped

1 tablespoon fresh lime juice

1 teaspoon Dijon mustard (optional)

1 teaspoon fine sea salt

½ teaspoon freshly ground black pepper

In a large bowl, combine the tomatoes, green pepper, red onion, oil, garlic, habanero, lime juice, mustard (if using), salt, and pepper, and fold together with a large spoon. Taste and adjust the seasoning as needed. Serve cold or at room temperature. (Store the sauce in a resealable jar with a tight-fitting lid in the refrigerator for up to 3 days.)

GHANAIAN SHITO SAUCE

MAKES ABOUT 2½ CUPS

If you ever have a Ghanaian friend over for dinner, well, they'll be really happy they came over to sample your version of their beloved condiment. This staple requires a bit of time to cook, but it's well worth the effort: Make it once, and it keeps for months. Everyone's shito tastes a little bit different, but the key is the funky flavor you get from the fermented ingredients. My shito is made with dried shrimp and smoked fish; you can make it with one or the other, but if you do use only one, make sure you double the portion. Shito sauce is usually served very spicy, but if you can't stand the heat, it can be prepared without any chili and will still be delicious. The slow cooking method allows the ingredients to blend and darken to its signature black color gradually without burning. It's also what gives shito a long shelf life of up to two months in the refrigerator.

NOTE: The dried smoked fish is usually catfish, shad, sardines, or herring.

3 cups chopped red onion

2 cups peanut oil, plus more as needed

1 cup chopped green bell pepper

6 tablespoons tomato purée

3 tablespoons grated fresh ginger

4 garlic cloves, very finely chopped

1 tablespoon chopped fresh thyme

½ cup ground dried shrimp or crayfish (see page 34) or 2 tablespoons fish sauce

½ cup crumbled smoked fish (skin off and bones removed; see Note)

1 tablespoon chili powder or cayenne (optional)

1 teaspoon fine sea salt

1 teaspoon freshly ground black pepper

In a blender or food processor, combine the red onion, oil, green pepper, tomato purée, ginger, garlic, and thyme and blend until smooth. Transfer the mixture to a medium pot and cook over medium heat, stirring frequently with a wooden spoon to avoid scorching, until bubbly and the moisture evaporates, about 30 minutes. Add the dried shrimp, smoked fish, and chili powder (if using). Reduce the heat to low and continue cooking until the oil is almost completely absorbed but not overly dry, another hour, stirring often to prevent burning (if the mixture seems to be drying out too much, add more oil, 2 to 3 tablespoons at a time, to keep it a pesto-like consistency). Season with the salt and pepper and continue stirring occasionally until the mixture turns a dark black color, about 30 minutes to 1 hour. Remove from the heat and allow to cool to room temperature. (Store the sauce in a resealable jar with a tight-fitting lid in the refrigerator until ready to use, for up to 2 months.)

WEST AFRICAN PIRI-PIRI SAUCE

MAKES ABOUT 2 CUPS

Chili peppers are not native to Africa. This now-ubiquitous plant made its way to the continent from Latin America with Portuguese settlers in the late fifteenth century. *Piri-piri* is the Swahili word for the African bird's eye chili, and this recipe is the tangy hot sauce you wish you always had as part of your repertoire. It has that perfect combination of spice and acidity and aromatics, without which one's meal would be just a little less exciting. My go-to version is spicy, tangy, joyous, and so invigorating that it makes me want to dance.

½ cup olive or vegetable oil

1 large red bell pepper, chopped

1 cup seeded and chopped habanero, Scotch bonnet, African bird's eye, or Thai chilies

½ cup chopped yellow onion

4 garlic cloves, chopped

1 bay leaf

1 teaspoon smoked paprika

½ cup chopped fresh cilantro

¼ cup chopped fresh basil

2 tablespoons red wine vinegar

1 tablespoon fresh lemon juice

1 teaspoon fine sea salt

REVIVING THE FLAVORS OF YOUR SAUCES AND STEWS

Sometimes, when you cook something for a long time on the stove, the intensity of the spices can get a bit diluted. This is just an inevitable side effect of slow cooking (not too dissimilar from the natural process of aging that begets any living, breathing organism). I want to share a little secret that my mother taught me: If you feel like the flavors are fading in your pot, just put a few drops of vinegar or a nice squeeze of lemon or lime into the mix to revive the flavors. This little acidic punch is the equivalent of a cold shower after a long day: instantly refreshing. Give it a try on one of these recipes, like the West African Red Sauce (page 51), the Mustard-Onion Relish (page 47), or on anything else that needs a little brightening.

In a large skillet, heat 2 tablespoons of the oil over medium-high heat. Add the bell pepper, habanero, onion, garlic, bay leaf, and paprika, and cook, stirring occasionally with a wooden spoon, until the vegetables are softened, about 10 minutes.

Allow the pepper mixture to cool, then add it to a blender or food processor, along with the cilantro, basil, vinegar, lemon juice, and salt. Process until the mixture has reached a smooth, saucelike consistency. (You may leave the sauce slightly chunky, if you prefer.) Drizzle the remaining ¼ cup plus 2 tablespoons oil on top of the sauce and stir to incorporate. Serve as a hot sauce to spice up any meal. (Store the sauce in a resealable jar with a tight-fitting lid in the refrigerator for up to 1 week.)

EVERYDAY HOT PEPPER KANI SAUCE

MAKES 2 CUPS

Are you ready to meet your new favorite hot condiment? This is called a sauce, but it's actually a condiment served on the side of various dishes. Scotch bonnets are a must-have in any Senegalese kitchen, and kani sauce is the perfect way to make sure you have this extremely hot chili in a friendly form that's ready to deploy. If you don't want to use Scotch bonnets, you can substitute a habanero, a close cousin of the infamous fiery chili that is a little bit easier on the taste buds. In moderation, this sauce's heat helps open up the pores on the tongue, making whatever it is served with taste better. Used in excess, you'll get the opposite effect: Your taste buds will go numb, and you'll be reaching for that water glass after every bite! So, my recommendation with this kani sauce, as with anything in life, is don't be afraid to treat yourself, but don't go overboard!

2 tablespoons vegetable oil

1 cup chopped yellow onion

1 garlic clove, chopped

3 medium plum tomatoes, chopped

1 tablespoon tomato paste

1 Scotch bonnet (or 2 to 3 for a spicier blend) or habanero chili, chopped

1 bay leaf

1 teaspoon fine sea salt

1 teaspoon freshly ground black pepper

In a large sauté pan, heat the oil over medium heat. Add the onion and garlic and cook, stirring frequently with a wooden spoon, until the garlic is fragrant and the onion is translucent, about 5 minutes. Stir in the chopped tomatoes, tomato paste, Scotch bonnet, bay leaf, salt, and pepper. Reduce the heat to low and continue cooking, stirring frequently to avoid scorching, until thickened and reduced to a loose paste, about 10 minutes. Taste and adjust the seasoning as needed, then let cool to room temperature before serving. (Store the sauce in a resealable jar with a tight-fitting lid in the refrigerator for up to 2 weeks.)

MY FRIEND, THE SCOTCH BONNET

I like chili peppers of all kinds, but the Scotch bonnet holds a special place in my heart—and on my plate. On the scale of mild to mouth-on-fire, it definitely errs on the side of pretty darn spicy, but that's not the only reason I love it. West Africans use Scotch bonnets not just to add a kick and flavor to our dishes but almost like a reusable topping that we place on our meals to infuse its sweet and spicy aroma into whatever we might be eating at that moment. It's a touch hotter than a habanero and has distinctly aromatic notes that make it the perfect companion to African and African-inspired flavors like those found in South America and the Caribbean. The most dangerous part is the seeds, so if you don't want to be extinguishing fire in your mouth all day, you can remove them and enjoy all the benefits without the risks.

SWEET PEPPER "EGUSI" SAUCE

MAKES 4 CUPS

Let me introduce you to a very important friend to every Nigerian home chef: the egusi seed. The seed comes from the egusi gourd, which looks a lot like the common watermelon but is not nearly as tasty. The fruit itself is so bitter that nobody eats it, but the egusi seed is a staple ingredient in our cuisine. Similar to pumpkin seeds but with a creamier, nuttier flavor profile, it's an excellent source of antioxidants and potassium, and is commonly used to make soups and sauces, and to top vegetable and meat dishes. If you're fortunate enough to find egusi in your local market, then by all means use it. In this recipe, I use pumpkin seeds as a substitute and combine them with roasted red bell peppers for a tantalizingly sweet, Spanish romesco-like sauce that you'll want to eat over and over again. You'll need this sauce to make the roasted kabocha on page 209. It also pairs well with cooked chicken or fish.

2 red bell peppers, halved

1 medium red onion, cut into quarters

4 large garlic cloves

½ cup raw shelled pumpkin seeds or egusi (see page 35)

1 (14.5-ounce) can crushed tomatoes

1 teaspoon rice or white vinegar

1 teaspoon fine sea salt, plus more as needed

1 teaspoon freshly ground black pepper, plus more as needed

½ cup sustainably sourced red palm oil (see page 31)

2 cups vegetable stock or water

2 teaspoons dawadawa powder (see page 34) or 1 tablespoon fish sauce (optional)

Preheat the oven to 425°F. Line a sheet pan with aluminum foil.

On the foil-lined sheet pan, place the bell peppers, red onion, and garlic. Roast until the bell peppers begin to char, about 25 minutes. Allow the peppers to cool until they are easy to handle. Using your hands, peel off and discard the skin from the peppers.

In a small dry skillet, toast the pumpkin seeds over medium heat until fragrant and slightly brown, about 7 minutes (careful that they don't burn).

In a blender or food processor, add the roasted pepper mixture, tomatoes, vinegar, pumpkin seeds, salt, and pepper. Purée on high until mostly smooth.

In a large pot, heat the palm oil over medium-high. Add the puréed mixture and stir to combine. Cook until it begins to sputter, 1 to 2 minutes. Stir in the vegetable stock. Bring to a boil over high heat, reduce the heat to low, and cook until combined, about 5 minutes. Add the dawadawa powder (if using), reduce the heat to low, then simmer, stirring occasionally with a wooden spoon to avoid clumps, until thickened, about 10 minutes. Taste and adjust the seasoning with a little more salt and pepper as needed. (Cool and store the sauce in a resealable jar with a tight-fitting lid in the refrigerator for up to 2 weeks.)

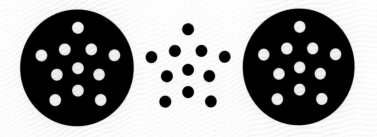

BACK-TO-BAHIA TOMATO-COCONUT-LIME SAUCE

MAKES ABOUT 4 CUPS

I love this sauce for many reasons. The unique combination of delightful flavors—from the savory red palm oil and sweet coconut to the perfectly tangy lime and acidity of the tomato—bursts with summery joy. It's also incredibly versatile. You can cook any type of seafood (shrimp, scallops, fish) directly in this sauce, or just pour it over rice or vegetables. It also tells an interesting story of how dishes from West Africa can evolve and translate into delicacies now representative of other parts of the world: This dish was inspired by bobó de camarão, a dish that hails from Bahia, the Brazilian state that boasts the biggest African population outside of the African continent. The original dish is cooked with shrimp, but I like keeping it vegetarian and turn it into a sauce, which gives me so much more flexibility with how it's served.

1 pound peeled fresh or frozen cassava, cut into 2-inch chunks

2 tablespoons sustainably sourced red palm oil (see page 31)

1 medium yellow onion, diced

1 medium green bell pepper, diced

2 medium plum tomatoes, coarsely chopped (about 1 cup)

2 garlic cloves, minced

1 (½-inch) piece of fresh ginger, peeled and grated

2 cups vegetable stock or water, plus more as needed

1½ cups or 1 (13.5-ounce) can unsweetened full-fat coconut milk

1 Scotch bonnet or habanero chili, seeded and finely chopped (optional)

1½ teaspoons fine sea salt

1 teaspoon freshly ground black pepper

½ cup fresh cilantro leaves, for serving

1 lime, cut into wedges, for serving

In a saucepan, add the cassava pieces and enough water to cover the cassava by 2 inches. Bring to a boil over high heat, then reduce the heat to medium and simmer until the cassava begins to split and is easily pierced with a fork, about 20 minutes. Drain and allow to cool slightly. (Sometimes the cassava comes with a hard fibrous core at its center. If so, remove with the tip of a knife and discard.) Transfer the cassava to a large bowl and mash with a fork or a potato masher until it becomes a chunky purée. Set aside.

Rinse and wipe out the saucepan in which the cassava was cooked. In the saucepan, heat 1 tablespoon of the oil over medium-high heat. Add the onion and bell pepper and sauté until soft, about 5 minutes. Add the tomatoes and sauté until soft and the tomatoes' juices release, another 5 minutes. Add the garlic and ginger and continue cooking for another minute. Add the vegetable stock. Simmer until the liquid is reduced by half, about 10 minutes. Stir in the coconut milk, Scotch bonnet (if using), mashed cassava, and the remaining 1 tablespoon oil. Let the mixture come to a simmer, stirring often with a wooden spoon. Add more stock as needed to thin the sauce if it's too thick. Season with the salt and pepper. Serve hot over rice or grilled vegetables, topped with the cilantro and the lime wedges on the side. (Cool and store the sauce in a resealable jar with a tight-fitting lid in the refrigerator for up to 1 week.)

GBEGIRI WITH BLACK-EYED PEAS AND RED PALM OIL

MAKES 4 CUPS

Although it is called a soup in Nigeria, this hearty, velvety concoction looks more like a sauce. It is the recipe that takes me back to Lagos every time I make it. Also known as buka soup, in Nigeria you can find gbegiri almost anywhere, from upscale restaurants to street-side food vendors. Some people make it by combining the black-eyed peas with beef bones and any fresh vegetables they have on hand. The version I introduce here, which uses black-eyed peas, still does the classic favorite justice.

2 cups dried black-eyed peas

1 cup chopped yellow onion

1 tablespoon ground dried shrimp (see page 34; optional)

2 teaspoons freshly ground black pepper, plus more as needed

1 teaspoon dawadawa powder (see page 34) or 1 tablespoon fish sauce

½ teaspoon sea salt, plus more as needed

1 tablespoon sustainably sourced red palm oil (see page 31)

Fufu (page 228) or cooked rice, for serving

In a large bowl, soak the black-eyed peas in water to cover for about 15 minutes.

In a blender or food processor, add the drained peas in small batches and pulse, being careful not to turn them into a purée, for 5 seconds each (see page 66) just to roughly break them up. Transfer each batch of the chopped peas to a second large bowl before repeating with the remaining peas. Once all the peas are in the second bowl, fill it with warm water so it covers all the peas by at least 2 inches. Rub the peas between your hands, a small handful at a time, so that the skins float to the top. Repeat several times until most of the skins come off the peas. Scoop away the floating skins with a slotted spoon or mesh strainer, or pour the peas into a colander and sort through the remaining peas to remove all the skins.

In a large saucepan, add the peeled peas and 5 cups of water. Bring to a boil over high heat, then add the onion, dried shrimp (if using), pepper, dawadawa, and salt. Reduce the heat to low and simmer until the peas are very tender, 30 to 45 minutes. Mash with a potato masher or process in a blender until smooth.

In a small sauté pan, heat the oil over medium-high heat until hot, about 2 minutes. Transfer the oil into the pan with the mashed bean mixture and stir to combine. It should have a semi-fluid consistency and coat the back of a spoon. Reduce the heat to medium and continue cooking, stirring occasionally, 5 more minutes. The gbegiri will turn a bright orange color. Taste and adjust the seasoning and serve piping hot with fufu or cooked rice. (If you are planning to save leftovers, keep in mind that the sauce will thicken over time. When reheating, add a few tablespoons of water if the mixture is too thick and stir to incorporate.)

PULSING AND PEELING THE PERFECT PEA

Preparing black-eyed peas for a successful cooking experience is a multistep process, but when done with the right attitude, it can be a welcome prelude to meal prep. I like to think of it as an opportunity to do a little meditative practice before the stovetop cooking begins. First, I soak the dried peas for about fifteen minutes in cold water to loosen the skins. Then, I pulse the peas in a blender for just a few seconds to break them—you don't want to purée them at all. This "shaking" of the peas helps separate the loosened skin from the peas themselves. Next comes the fun part: I immerse the peas in a bowl of water (you can use the same bowl as the initial soak), and I take a small number of beans and rub them gently between the palms of my hands. The skin, which has a lighter weight than the peas, separates and rises to the surface of the water. I repeat this rubbing process several times until most of the peas are skinless, saying to myself a mantra like "I am peeling the perfect pea." Then, I manually go through the rest to find any remaining peas that still have skins on them. The final step is to scoop out the floating skins and drain the peas.

SNACKS

NOSTALGIA-INDUCING TREATS

NOSTALGIA-INDUCING TREATS

SNACKS

I'm going to let you in on a little secret: I love snacking. I love it almost as much as I love sitting down to eat a full meal. By now it's almost standard fare around the world to sequence meals: breakfast, lunch, dinner. But when I was growing up, I used to snack all day. I snacked during recess. I built relationships with the snack vendors on my way home from school. My mom would give me change money that I'd promptly spend on a cup of thiakry, a sweet millet couscous with yogurt and dried fruits; fataya, a Lebanese meat-filled pastry; and paañ, ceviche-like marinated dried clams with chilies, lime, and onion.

In this chapter, you'll learn how to make snacks inspired by some of the most delectable and irresistible street foods from my childhood, like the Savory Chin Chin Crisps (page 74) from Togo and the Akara Chickpea Fritters (page 79) from Benin. These recipes come from all over West Africa, reminding us that we are all connected, all part of a sprawling and intersectional community that transcends colonial borders. I've modified these local favorites to be ready for cooking in the home kitchen and to be as casual or fancy as you need them to be—for example, whether you're munching Ndambe Nachos with Black-Eyed Peas and Butternut Squash (page 73) as a shared snack while watching TV or passing around Vegetable Pastels (page 84), inspired by a Cape Verdean snack, at the beginning of a sit-down dinner party.

SPICED BOILED PEANUTS

MAKES ABOUT 3 CUPS

Every family has its own version of that irresistible snack that people can't stop reaching for no matter how hard they try. These peanuts are our go-to favorite—and maybe they'll become yours, too, after you try them. They are incredibly simple to prepare and perfect as a predinner treat, with a cold beer on a hot summer day, or to sprinkle on top of a salad as a topping.

SAND, A DAKAR STREET VENDOR'S SECRET "ROASTING" TOOL

If you ever see a street vendor in Dakar cooking peanuts, you might notice that they're using sea sand at the bottom of their wok. This ingenious technique, sometimes called hot-sand roasting, is used for dry cooking peanuts. The sand conducts heat swiftly and evenly, resulting in a faster dehydration process that creates the perfect crunch. And because Dakar is a seaside city, sand is literally everywhere—not a difficult commodity to acquire. If you have access to clean sea sand, you, too, can try this. Simply pour clean sea sand into a wok until the wok is half full, turn the heat on your stovetop to high, and stir the sand with a large slotted spoon until the heat is evenly distributed throughout the sand. Then, drop shelled peanuts into the sand while stirring, and watch them roast to delicious perfection. You'll know they're ready when the skin dries up and starts to split, and the peanuts are crunchy when you bite into them. You don't have to worry about the sand sticking to the peanuts because dry beach sand, when heated, eliminates all humidity, and the sand and peanuts stay quite separate. Once your peanuts are cooked, sift out the sand and you have yourself an amazing, Dakar-style sand-cooked street snack!

1 pound shelled raw peanuts
¼ cup fine sea salt
1 tablespoon ground ginger
2 teaspoons cayenne pepper
1 teaspoon garlic powder
Finely chopped parsley, for garnish

In a large bowl, soak the peanuts in water to cover for 4 hours, then rinse and drain.

In a large pot, add 2 quarts of water, the peanuts, and salt. Bring the water to a rolling boil over high heat, then add the ginger, cayenne, and garlic powder. Reduce the heat to low to let it simmer, cover, and cook until the peanuts are soft and buttery, 30 minutes to 1 hour. Allow to cool in the liquid, then drain. Top with chopped parsley, if desired. Serve as a snack as is or with a cocktail, or use as a topping for salads. (Store the peanuts in a resealable jar with a tight-fitting lid in the refrigerator for up to 1 week.)

NDAMBE NACHOS
WITH BLACK-EYED PEAS AND BUTTERNUT SQUASH

SERVES 8 ㅅㅅㅅㅅㅅㅅㅅㅅ

I would be remiss if I didn't include a West African take on nachos, a very popular party food in America. Many people have already adapted this Mexican/American snack, heaping all types of ingredients on top of corn chips, with versions ranging from heavy and filling (beef, beans, sour cream, and more) to simple and elegant (tomatoes, avocados, and onions). This one is somewhere in between. The black-eyed peas and butternut squash in the ndambe certainly give it some heartiness, but it's also completely vegetarian and incredibly nourishing. My recommendation, of course, is to make it with Yolélé fonio chips (see page 18), which are delicious and healthy and come in multiple flavors if you want to add some fun.

1 (10-ounce) bag of your favorite chips (I recommend Yolélé fonio chips or tortilla chips)

1 pound sharp Cheddar cheese, coarsely shredded (about 4½ cups)

4 cups Senegalese Ndambe Peasant Stew (page 210)

¼ cup Moyo Sauce Goes with Everything (page 56), for serving

2 tablespoons chopped fresh flat-leaf parsley, for serving

Preheat the oven to 350°F.

Spread the chips over a large sheet pan. Sprinkle half of the grated cheese over the chips. Sprinkle the ndambe over the chips and cheese. Sprinkle the remaining cheese on top of the ndambe. Bake until the cheese is melted, about 10 minutes. Top with the moyo sauce and scatter the chopped parsley over the hot nachos. Serve hot.

SAVORY CHIN CHIN CRISPS

SERVES 4 TO 6 ᎪᎪᎪᎪ

These crispy treats are about to become your new favorite homemade snack. As a kid growing up in Dakar, every day I looked forward to pit stops at the Togolese street vendors who sold delightful, fun-to-say-out-loud bites out of busy roadside kiosks to schoolkids—chin chin pastry crisps, akara chickpea fritters, and pof pof beignets. The chin chin I remember from my childhood was sweet and the size of small pebbles, but my version is savory and shaped into strips, with some spices to give it a little kick.

4 cups all-purpose flour, plus more for sprinkling

¾ cup extra-virgin olive oil

2 tablespoons finely chopped or grated yellow onion

2 garlic cloves, finely chopped

1 teaspoon fine sea salt

½ teaspoon freshly ground black pepper

¼ teaspoon cayenne pepper

1 large egg

Vegetable oil, for frying

¼ cup yellow onion slices, to season the oil

Sift the flour into a large bowl. Using your fingers, mix the olive oil into the flour until it has the texture of a coarse meal. Add the chopped onion, garlic, salt, pepper, and cayenne. Mix well.

In a small bowl, combine ½ cup of water and the egg, and whisk. Slowly add the egg mixture to the flour mixture and mix with your hands until the dough holds together. Knead the dough until smooth and elastic, about 5 minutes, then divide into 2 pieces.

Sprinkle your work surface and a large sheet pan with flour. Using a rolling pin, roll one of the dough pieces to about ¼-inch thickness. Fold the dough in half and cut it into 1-inch-wide strips. Unfold the strips and cut them crosswise into 3-inch-long rectangles. Set aside on the prepared sheet pan. Repeat with the remaining dough.

Line a large platter with paper towels and set aside.

In a large heavy-bottomed pot or deep skillet, add enough vegetable oil so it goes about 3 inches up the sides. Heat the oil over medium-high heat until it reaches 350°F. Add the onion slices to the oil and cook until they are burned, about 3 minutes. Remove with a slotted spoon or tongs and discard. Cooking in batches so as not to overcrowd the pot, transfer the pieces of dough to the hot oil and fry, turning once, until golden brown on both sides, 1 to 2 minutes. Transfer the crisps to the paper towel–lined platter to drain. Serve immediately while warm or at room temperature. (The chips can be made in advance and kept in the freezer to reheat later in the oven at 350°F for about 5 minutes.)

SEASONING YOUR FRYING OIL

Seasoning frying oil is one of those tricks used by West African mamas to make fried food taste even better. In the Savory Chin Chin Crisps recipe (opposite), I use the most common method, which to put a few onion slices into the oil as it heats up in the pan, and let the slices burn before discarding them. This infuses the oil with a sweet, caramelized aroma, without adding any weight to the dish. (Alternatively, flavor your oil with your favorite spices or herbs by using the same method.)

GREEN MORINGA COCONUT DIP

MAKES ABOUT 2 CUPS

Move over, creamy spinach! There's a new dip in town, and it's about to take over potluck parties all over America. I love this dip because, like everything in this book, it is a healthy alternative to a favorite snack that you can eat as much as you want of without getting that heavy, "Ohhh, I ate waaaay too much" feeling afterward. The moringa has a special earthy flavor to it that you can't quite get from other green dips. Paired with the cilantro, parsley, garlic, and onion, it takes on a really nice, zingy-cozy feeling that will keep you coming back.

1 cup peeled, cubed russet potatoes (1-inch cubes)

1½ cups or 1 (13.5-ounce) can unsweetened full-fat coconut milk

1 cup chopped yellow onion

3 garlic cloves, finely chopped

1 tablespoon grated fresh ginger

2 tablespoons moringa powder (see page 35) or 1 cup moringa leaves or spinach

1 teaspoon fine sea salt

½ teaspoon freshly ground black pepper

½ cup chopped fresh cilantro

½ cup chopped fresh flat-leaf parsley

2 tablespoons fresh lemon juice

1 teaspoon seeded and finely chopped habanero or Scotch bonnet chili

In a medium pot, add the potatoes and enough water to cover the potatoes by 2 inches. Bring to a boil over high heat. Reduce the heat to low and simmer until the potatoes are tender and easily pierced with a fork, about 15 minutes. Drain, discard the water, and return the cooked potatoes to the pot.

Add the coconut milk, onion, garlic, and ginger to the potatoes. Bring to a boil over high heat. Reduce the heat to low and simmer until the mixture is combined, 5 more minutes. Add the moringa, salt, and pepper, and stir with a wooden spoon to incorporate, about 5 more minutes. Remove from the heat and allow the mixture to cool completely, at least 10 minutes.

Place the cooled mixture in a blender or food processor. Add the cilantro, parsley, lemon juice, and habanero, and blend on the highest setting until the mixture is smooth and has the consistency of thick whipped cream. Let cool to room temperature before serving. (Store in the refrigerator in an airtight container for up to 2 days.)

AKARA CHICKPEA FRITTERS

MAKES 15 FRITTERS

These light and fluffy fritters rank among my favorite street foods ever. In Dakar, they are usually prepared with black-eyed peas, but I find chickpeas to be so much easier to peel, and the result is just as wonderful. This is the perfect appetizer or snack to pair with kani sauce or to enjoy whenever you have the craving for a salty crunchy snack.

THE GINGER OIL TESTING METHOD

This chapter has a lot of fun, delicious fried foods, but if you don't have a thermometer, you might be wondering, How in the world will I know when the oil is hot enough, but not too hot? Here's a tried-and-true, age-old West African trick that is especially useful if you're already cooking with ginger: Shave a few tiny slivers off a piece of ginger using a paring knife or vegetable peeler. When you suspect that the oil is reaching optimal frying temperature, drop one of the ginger slivers into the oil. If the oil is hot enough, the ginger will sizzle and rise to the top. If it's not, the ginger will sink. If the oil is too hot, it will splatter and the ginger will burn. If this happens, simply remove the pan from the heat for thirty seconds or so, and then try again.

Another trick is to stick a wooden skewer, chopstick, or spoon handle into the oil. If the bubbles are tiny, steady, and float to the surface, that means that the oil is ready. If the bubbles are vigorous, it means that your oil is too hot and you should reduce the heat and let the oil cool a bit.

2 cups dried chickpeas

1 cup chopped yellow onion

1 (1-inch) piece of fresh ginger, peeled and coarsely chopped

1 teaspoon baking powder

1 teaspoon fine sea salt

Vegetable oil, for frying

2 cups Everyday Hot Pepper Kani Sauce (page 59)

In a large bowl, soak the chickpeas in water to cover overnight, then drain.

Hull the chickpeas by rubbing them between your hands to remove the skin. (This peeling process can be done days in advance.) In a blender or food processor, add the peeled chickpeas, onion, ginger, baking powder, and salt, and pulse on the highest setting, adding ¼ to ½ cup of water, 1 tablespoon at a time, to facilitate the blending process. Blend until the batter is thick and smooth. Transfer the mixture to a large bowl.

Right before frying, use a whisk or an electric hand whisk to whip the batter for about 2 minutes to increase its volume. (The more air that is incorporated during the whipping, the fluffier the fritters will be.)

In a small saucepan, heat 2 inches of oil over medium-high heat until it's hot, using the Ginger Oil Testing Method (see left) to determine whether the oil is ready. Using a tablespoon to scoop the batter, carefully spoon it into the oil. (Fritters will puff up into round balls.) Using a slotted spoon, turn the fritters in the oil to ensure they have an even, golden brown coloring on all sides, 3 to 4 minutes. Once the fritters are cooked, scoop them out of the oil and drain them on a paper towel. Serve as a snack with the kani sauce.

SMOKY BLACK-EYED PEA HUMMUS

MAKES ABOUT 2 CUPS

Beans and peas are at the nutritional and social foundations of nearly every culture. They symbolize health, wealth, good fortune—basically anything positive and nurturing. Black-eyed peas were originally cultivated in West Africa and were introduced to the American South through the Middle Passage. Today, they are served on New Year's Day in many African American and Southern homes alongside collard greens to bring good luck and money in the coming year.

A traditional way of preparing black-eyed peas in West Africa is by pounding it into a dough to create classics like akara and moi moi. This dish riffs on the technique by mashing cooked black-eyed peas with a wooden spoon and uses smoked paprika, which gives it a distinctly musky flavor that I love. This dip is great served alongside crackers, fonio chips (see page 18), rice, veggies—basically, however you want to spice up your life with this joyful blend is okay by me. It also requires almost no cooking skills, kids love it, and if you have any left over, you can store it in the fridge for up to a week. A clear win-win-win-win!

2 tablespoons extra-virgin olive oil

½ cup chopped white onion

3 garlic cloves, chopped

1 (15.5 ounce) can black-eyed peas, rinsed and drained

½ teaspoon smoked paprika

½ teaspoon dried rosemary

¼ teaspoon dried thyme

½ cup vegetable stock or water

2 tablespoons sustainably sourced red palm oil (see page 31)

1 teaspoon fine sea salt

1 teaspoon freshly ground black pepper

2 tablespoons Garlicky Parsley Rof (page 49), for serving

Cayenne pepper, for serving

In a medium saucepan, heat the olive oil over medium heat. Add the onion and garlic and sauté, stirring occasionally with a wooden spoon, until the onion is translucent, 2 to 3 minutes. Add the black-eyed peas, paprika, rosemary, and thyme, and continue to cook until heated through, 2 to 3 minutes. Stir in the vegetable stock, palm oil, salt, and pepper, then lightly smash the beans with the wooden spoon until the mixture has a coarse but spreadable texture. (Alternatively, you can pulse in a blender or food processor.) Allow to cool to room temperature. Stir in the rof and a sprinkle of cayenne on top. (Store the dip in a resealable jar with a tight-fitting lid in the refrigerator for up to 1 week.)

BANANA POF POFS
WITH CILANTRO AND SCALLIONS

MAKES ABOUT 12 FRITTERS

This savory, gluten-free rendition of the beignet is oh-so crispy, crunchy, tasty, and packed with vitamins and folate. It's also a great recipe to try when you have overripe bananas. It's inspired by a Cameroonian dish called pof pofs or beignet banana, in which ripe bananas are first mixed with cassava. In my version, I included scallions and cilantro for an additional kick of flavor. The dough is then "slow-fried" at a lower temperature for the perfect texture—tender inside, while caramelized and crisp on the outside. (Slow-frying is often used for starchy foods and it's the way to go here!) These fritters can be enjoyed on their own or dipped in kani sauce or shito sauce. My daughter, Naia, likes to dip hers in ketchup. My wife, Lisa, dips hers in Kewpie mayonnaise. Whatever works for you, works for me.

2 cups peeled, cored, and grated fresh or frozen cassava (from about ½ pound)

2 overripe bananas, peeled

½ cup finely ground cornmeal

2 tablespoons finely sliced scallions

1 tablespoon chopped fresh cilantro

1 tablespoon fine sea salt

Vegetable oil, for frying

Everyday Hot Pepper Kani Sauce (page 59) or Ghanaian Shito Sauce (page 57), for serving

Tightly squeeze the grated cassava in a clean kitchen towel or cheesecloth to remove excess moisture. Place the cassava in a medium bowl.

In a large bowl, mash the bananas into a paste. Add the cassava and mix well. Add the cornmeal, scallions, cilantro, and salt. Mash well to combine into a uniform dough, adding a few drops of water, if needed, to help the dough hold its shape. Using a small cookie scoop or your hands, shape the dough into little oval balls about 1 inch in size, and line them up on a platter.

Line a sheet pan with paper towels and set aside.

In a large heavy-bottomed pot or deep skillet, add enough oil so that it goes about 3 inches up the sides. Heat the oil over medium-high heat until it reaches 350°F, or until it makes a sizzling sound when you drop a small piece of the batter in it. Once the oil is hot, reduce the heat to low, then carefully drop the balls, one by one, into the oil, making sure not to

overcrowd the pot. Once the fritters have reached a nice golden brown color on one side, 4 to 5 minutes, turn them with a slotted spoon and cook until golden brown on the other side, another 4 to 5 minutes. Transfer the fritters to the paper towel–lined sheet pan and cover them with aluminum foil to keep warm. Increase the heat to medium-high until the oil temperature reaches 350°F again, then reduce the heat to low and repeat with the remaining batter. Serve immediately with the sauce of your choice.

VEGETABLE PASTELS

MAKES ABOUT 8 PASTELS

This outstanding snack originates from the Cape Verde islands, which are located off the western coast of Africa, in the Atlantic Ocean. It is a popular street food in Dakar, some four hundred plus miles away. Outside of New England and, of course, Cape Verde itself, Senegal has one of the largest communities of Cape Verdeans, who migrated there in the 1920s in search of job opportunities. We see influences of their culture and cuisine throughout the city, like in these crispy vegetable-filled bites. I make this snack often for parties because they're a clear crowd favorite, and I suggest you do, too. I use empanada dough because it's easy to find in the frozen food aisle at most supermarkets.

2 tablespoons olive or vegetable oil

½ cup diced yellow onion

2 garlic cloves, chopped

1 cup cooked or canned black-eyed peas, rinsed and drained

1 green bell pepper, diced

1 red bell pepper, diced

½ cup chopped plum tomatoes

½ bunch of fresh cilantro, roughly chopped

1 bay leaf

2 teaspoons fine sea salt

½ teaspoon freshly ground black pepper

8 disks of frozen empanada dough

Vegetable oil, for frying

Everyday Hot Pepper Kani Sauce (page 59) or Garlicky Parsley Rof (page 49), for serving (optional)

In a large skillet, heat the olive oil over medium-high heat. Add the onion and sauté until soft but not brown, about 3 minutes. Add the garlic and continue to sauté. Add the black-eyed peas, green and red bell peppers, tomatoes, cilantro (leaves and stems), bay leaf, salt, and pepper, and cook over medium heat, stirring often, until the liquid is reduced, about 3 minutes. Turn off the heat and allow the vegetable mixture to cool to room temperature. Using a fork or masher, mash the black-eyed peas into the vegetables to form a compact mixture. Set aside.

Lay the dough on a sheet pan. Using a small spoon, fill the center of each dough with 2 tablespoons of the vegetable mixture. With your fingers, enclose the vegetables by folding one corner over the other to form a semicircle, then pinch the edges. Seal all the way around with a fork.

In a large heavy-bottomed pot or deep skillet, add enough vegetable oil so it goes about 3 inches up the sides. Heat the oil over medium-high heat until it reaches 350°F. Gently drop the pastels into the hot oil, being careful not to overcrowd the pot. Fry until nicely golden brown, 3 to 5 minutes per side. Transfer the pastels to a paper towel–lined sheet pan to drain, then serve hot on their own or with sauce. (Alternatively, these pastels can be baked on a lightly greased sheet pan, with their tops brushed with olive oil, at 350°F until the crust turns brown and crispy, about 20 minutes.)

PIERRE'S PUMPKIN-PEANUT RICE BALLS

MAKES ABOUT 12 BALLS

Many food cultures have a favorite rice ball treat. Where Lisa grew up in Japan, kids eat onigiri (short-grain rice balls wrapped in seaweed) for lunch almost every day. In Ghana, the Hausa people make a popular rice ball known as omo tuo, typically made using jasmine rice cooked in extra water for a softer texture. This recipe is for my very own signature rice balls (hence the name of the dish), which have a distinctly West African flavor thanks to the peanut and pumpkin. Serve them with mafé sauce or okra with tomatoes, or eat them on their own, Japanese-style.

1 cup Japanese short-grain rice, rinsed and drained

1 teaspoon fine sea salt

1 cup cooked and puréed pumpkin or canned purée

1 cup coarsely chopped roasted peanuts

Mafé Peanut Sauce (page 50) or Okra with Tomatoes (page 190), for serving (optional)

In a large pot, combine the rice, 2½ cups of water, and the salt, and bring to a boil over high heat. Reduce the heat to low, cover, and simmer until the water has almost all evaporated and the rice is soft, 20 minutes. Remove the lid from the pot and continue cooking, using a wooden spoon to knead the rice until mashed and sticky, another 10 minutes. Turn off the heat and allow the rice to cool slightly. Add the pumpkin purée to the cooked rice. Using a potato masher or a wooden spoon, mash the rice and pumpkin together until the texture is smooth. Stir in the peanuts.

Wet your hands with cold water and then scoop up enough of the rice mixture to shape into balls the size of a golf ball. Squeeze each ball tightly with your hands. Place on a platter, slightly covered with aluminum foil to keep warm. Repeat the process, regularly wetting your hands with cold water to prevent the rice from sticking to your palms. Serve immediately with mafé or okra (if using).

To store, allow the rice balls to cool to room temperature, then cover tightly with plastic wrap and refrigerate for up to 3 days or freeze for up to 3 months. To reheat, remove the plastic from the rice balls, wrap each one loosely in a damp paper towel, and microwave on high for at least 1 minute, adding more time in 10-second increments as needed until hot.

MEAT

SIMPLE COMFORT
FOODS

SIMPLE COMFORT FOODS

MEAT

Meat is not an absolute necessity to make a delicious West African meal, but some of my best memories of love expressed through food include delectable preparations of chicken, lamb, and beef. When I was growing up in Senegal, meat was reserved for special occasions. We often ate around a shared bowl in which grains, beans, and veggies were the main ingredients. If there was meat, it was in smaller portions, and always at the center of the bowl, to be divided up among us by mom. The meat at the center was where our eager fingers, shared joy, and family love all met.

Here, I bring you simple, meat-based comfort foods—ones with a West African spirit but intertwined with influences from all over the world—that pay homage to our families and loved ones. There's my Maman's Crispy Herb-Crusted Chicken (page 131) as well as Karaage-Style West African Fried Chicken (page 116), which combines both Lisa's and my cultures in perfect harmony. You'll make Aunt Marie's Sauce Feuille (page 110), the beloved dish my favorite aunt made for Lisa that made her a lifelong fan of West African cuisine. You'll make Papa's Famous Chicken Yassa Tacos (page 104), a Mexi–West African invention of my good friend Papa Mbengue, and Thiebou Yapp, the Ultimate Rice Pilaf (page 128), a paella-like rice dish made with lamb. Cooking these uncomplicated but delicious dishes will warm your heart, your home, and your spirit. (Because the part of West Africa where I grew up is mostly Muslim, I did not include any recipes that call for the use of pork. If you like, you can substitute pork for most of the meat dishes in this chapter, and they will taste just as great.)

In our home, we take the phrase "Cooking is a labor of love" quite literally. Lisa and I both come from cultures that aren't very openly affectionate or verbally profusive. Our parents and grandparents showed us love by presenting us with as much food as they could, not stopping until they were satisfied that they had done everything possible to make sure we wouldn't be hungry again for a very long time. While we both wholly believe in other ways of expressing love (Naia can attest to this because she is showered with hugs, kisses, "I love yous," and plenty of joy and praise at every turn of her beautiful evolution), we still embrace this value of showing love through food. Especially for me, as someone who has been working in kitchens my entire adult life, this comes most naturally. When I'm cooking for someone, I can feel the love emanating from deep in my bones, through my hands, and into the ingredients. When I'm not cooking for anyone in particular, somehow the food I end up with doesn't seem as fun or fulfilling.

This chapter is full of some of my favorite love letters. The layers of flavors packed into these meat-based curries, stews, and rice dishes intensify overnight. I always cook extra, so we can quickly reheat leftovers for lunch the next day, the day after that, and even the day after that. This turnkey approach to having food on the table every day means I get to spend more time playing with Naia. Food as love is a universal language that can be spoken by anyone. No translation required.

OXTAIL STEW

SERVES 4 TO 6 ♈♈♈♈

Once considered a humble cut of meat, oxtail today is like a long-lost friend you can run into anywhere, from the buffet lineup at an Afrocentric deli on Ninth Avenue in New York City to a deluxe tasting menu at a Michelin-starred restaurant. This recipe lets you take this melt-off-the-bone, finger-licking delight straight to your dining table. If oxtail is hard to find or out of your price range, this recipe also works great with goat.

1 cup dried red beans or 1 (15.5-ounce) can, rinsed and drained

4 pounds oxtail meat, trimmed of excess fat

1½ teaspoons fine sea salt, plus more as needed

½ teaspoon freshly ground black pepper, plus more as needed

2 tablespoons olive or vegetable oil

2 cups chopped yellow onion

6 garlic cloves, minced

2 tablespoons grated fresh ginger

¼ cup tomato paste

1 tablespoon soy sauce

½ teaspoon ground allspice

½ teaspoon smoked paprika

4 to 6 cups beef stock or water, as needed

4 sprigs of fresh thyme

2 bay leaves

1 habanero or Scotch bonnet chili, left whole (optional)

3 scallions, chopped, for serving

(RECIPE CONTINUES)

In a large pot, add the beans and 5 to 6 cups of water, and bring to a boil over high heat. Reduce the heat to low and cook at a simmer until the beans are soft, about 30 minutes, then drain. (Skip this step if you're using canned beans.)

In a large bowl, add the oxtail and season it with the salt and pepper.

In a large Dutch oven, heat the oil over medium-high heat. Once the oil is hot, add the oxtail and sear it in batches on all sides until browned. Transfer the oxtail to a plate and keep warm by covering it loosely with aluminum foil. Reduce the heat to medium, add the onions, and cook until softened, 3 to 5 minutes. Stir in the garlic and ginger, and cook, stirring continuously, for 1 minute. Stir in the tomato paste, soy sauce, allspice, and paprika. Cook until the paste browns slightly, 2 to 3 minutes.

Return the oxtail to the Dutch oven. Add enough beef stock to almost submerge the oxtail, then add the thyme sprigs, bay leaves, and habanero (if using); bring the mixture to a boil over high heat. Reduce the heat to its lowest setting, cover, and simmer until the meat is soft and tender, about 2 hours. Stir in the beans, being careful not to burst the habanero. Simmer, uncovered, until the liquid thickens, 10 more minutes.

Remove the thyme sprigs and bay leaves. Using a wooden spoon, partially mash some of the beans. Raise the heat to medium and stir until the liquid thickens some more, 2 to 3 minutes. Serve, garnished with the scallions. Place the habanero in a small dish on the side for the brave souls who like their food spicy.

EATING GOOD MEAT DOESN'T HAVE TO BE PRICEY

Over the years, we have all seen the cost of certain meats skyrocket. Take oxtail, for example: What used to be considered scrap meat has now been transformed into a delicacy, a pound of which can easily cost ten dollars. And while I always try to get organic, grass-fed meats straight from the butcher, I am also keenly aware that this is not possible for everyone, all the time. I'd like to share a philosophy here that I think will help. In most West African societies, we believe wholeheartedly in generosity and teranga (see page 13), but we also recognize the dangers and impracticalities of overeating. I love eating meat, but I try to err on the side of eating smaller portions of sustainably grown organic meats, versus stuffing my face with cheap overprocessed meats to the point of food coma (as I admittedly used to do in my youth). As I've grown in age and in wisdom (I hope!), I have found that cooking and eating mindfully is the best way to save money and stay healthy. In recent years, national superstores like Target and Safeway have also started stocking their shelves with organic, healthier alternatives to mass-produced, factory farm–fed animal produce. Efforts are being made all across the supply chain to ensure that good foods are being distributed more equitably. We still have a lot of work to do in terms of food equity, but I believe that if everyone becomes more conscious of their food choices, things will get better over time.

GINGER CHICKEN KEDJENOU
WITH EGGPLANT AND TOMATO

SERVES 4 ᴬᴬᴬᴬ

This elegant recipe from Côte d'Ivoire uses straightforward ingredients and a simple cooking method that requires no water and no oil. This allows the flavors to interact directly with one another to form a great-tasting dish that you'll no doubt want to cook again and again. Traditionally, the chicken is cooked in a clay pot and covered with banana leaves to prevent the steam from escaping. Here, all the ingredients are put into a Dutch oven with a lid and then cooked in a hot oven. The trick is to keep the lid on throughout the entire cooking process, which makes the ingredients bake *and* steam in their own juices. The compressed steam does a magical dance with the chicken and the other ingredients, resulting in the most flavorful broth and meat and vegetables with beautiful, soft textures. The recipe is easy to double, triple, or quadruple, and is delicious served over rice, atieke, or boiled cassava or yams. In this version, I've added spinach because Naia loves her greens! She also loves to lap up the pure and tasty chicken broth at the end of her meal. I prefer to remove the chicken skins, but it's fine to leave them on, too.

2 pounds bone-in chicken legs and thighs, skin on or off, separated (about 4 whole legs)

4 garlic cloves, chopped

2 scallions, finely chopped

1 tablespoon freshly ground black pepper

2 teaspoons fine sea salt

2 teaspoons chopped fresh ginger

1 teaspoon chopped fresh thyme

1 teaspoon smoked paprika

1 teaspoon cayenne pepper (optional)

1 large eggplant, halved and cut into 2-inch cubes

6 plum tomatoes (about 2 pounds), cut into 1-inch cubes

1 cup chopped yellow onion

1 cup coarsely chopped green bell pepper

1 cup coarsely chopped red bell pepper

1 bay leaf

8 ounces spinach (baby or young leaves), about 8 cups

Cooked rice, atieke (see page 35), or boiled cassava or yams, for serving

(RECIPE CONTINUES)

In a large bowl, add the chicken and season with the garlic, scallions, pepper, salt, ginger, thyme, paprika, and cayenne (if using). Cover and marinate in the refrigerator for at least 2 hours or overnight.

Preheat the oven to 350°F.

In a large Dutch oven or heavy-bottomed pot, place the marinated chicken and add the eggplant, tomatoes, onion, green and red bell peppers, and bay leaf. Mix well, cover, and cook in the oven without opening the lid for about 30 minutes. Remove the pot from the oven and lightly shake it once or twice, while still keeping the lid on, to prevent the ingredients from sticking to the bottom (you will need heatproof gloves or kitchen towels to hold and shake the hot pot). Return the pot to the oven and continue cooking until the chicken is cooked, the eggplant and bell peppers are soft, and enough juice has been released to form a broth, about 45 minutes.

Remove the pot from the oven, then fold in the spinach and stir until the spinach has wilted, about 1 minute. Serve hot with the rice or another starch of your choice.

BARBECUE, FROM AFRICA TO AMERICA

BARBECUE

Here in the United States, just hearing the word *barbecue* brings up images of hot summer afternoons with generous slabs of deliciously seasoned meat nestled closely together atop flaming charcoal in an open grill. Friends and family, letting loose to their favorite tunes, celebrating a special occasion—or no occasion at all. It's a unifying tradition that transcends culture, race, and class. Anyone can host a barbecue and enjoy doing so. It's one of our favorite ways to gather, because no matter how much or how little prep you do, grilling and eating together guarantees a good time for all. The spirit of teranga and hosting a barbecue are very closely related—in fact, I offer to you the very likely theory that they are one and the same. Every tradition is connected to other traditions.

The cultures and rituals of barbecue look somewhat different back in West Africa, but there are some fundamental similarities. Merriam-Webster defines the verb *barbecue* as "to roast or broil . . . on a rack or revolving spit over or before a source of heat (such as hot coals or a gas flame)." When I was growing up in Senegal, most home cooking was done using precisely this method, with a cooking tool called a fourneau. A fourneau is a small, wooden charcoal burner that consists of two pieces of metal, one on top of the other. The upper piece is a wok-like structure with an opening on the bottom covered with a metal grate that is designed to hold the burning charcoal while allowing air to circulate. The lower piece is connected to the base of the wok-like piece by a cylindrical chimney with a small opening at the bottom. The chimney's role is to facilitate the fanning of the fire and to collect the ashes. A fourneau is an incredibly useful kitchen tool. Place a pot or pan directly on the hot coals and it acts like a regular stove. Top with a metal grilling rack and it becomes a barbecue grill.

In Senegal, almost every household has a fourneau in the backyard, and it is used frequently to prepare meals. In Dakar, we always used wood charcoal when cooking on the fourneau to infuse a smoky fragrance and flavor to barbecued meats. My mother would throw all types of meat on ours to feed us kids and any other friends or relatives who happened our way for a meal. She'd cook lamb, guinea hens, chickens, whole fish— you name it. Some of my fondest childhood memories are of these meals.

In recent years, environmentalists have been campaigning to reduce the use of wood charcoal for cooking because it contributes to deforestation. As a result, some people have been switching to gas and electric stovetops, and others have replaced their traditional fourneaus with those designed to be more energy-efficient. I don't have a fourneau at my home in California, but I do have a good old Weber grill, and I use it on occasion to get the same smoky, slow-cooked effect on meats that I cook for my family for dinner.

The earliest recorded mention of barbecue in America is by George Washington in 1769. At the time, what we now know as barbecue was mainly cooked by captive Africans who used fire pits at large social gatherings that enslavers hosted on their plantations. The word *pitmaster*—still used at times to casually refer to the person manning the grill—was usually an older captive African who led the kitchen in preparing whole hogs and chickens for the event. The plantation owners, of course, were given the best cuts of meat, leaving the less desired parts of the animal, like the ribs, for the captives to eat later. These pitmasters passed on the techniques and traditions of barbecue to younger generations. They cultivated the art of slow cooking previously undesirable cuts of meat to tender deliciousness using a pit in the ground and makeshift tongs. (Of course, today, everyone considers these some of the best parts of a barbecue experience, proving yet again that recipes cultivated with love always prevail.)

Cooking meat in a pit is a tradition that takes me back to the motherland. There, cooks would dig a hole in the dirt ground, fortify the sides with bricks or stones, and then place some firewood in the pit. They then added a simple metal grate to cover the hole and, on top, the meat, often a whole lamb seasoned with salt, pepper, cumin, and other spices. The meat was covered with banana leaves and then a mound of dirt—to contain the steam and retain moisture. The animal would cook overnight, then be dug out the next day.

In West Africa, barbecue puts on many hats, depending on the occasion. If you happen to be visiting and are craving some grilled eats, here are a few types of places where you're sure to encounter the origins of barbecue.

SUYA JOINTS, THE ULTIMATE STREET FOOD EXPERIENCE

Suya joints can be found on street corners throughout West African cities like Lagos, Dakar, and Abidjan. Picture a dark, smoky shack with rustic wooden benches and vinyl-covered tables lined up against walls that have darkened over time because of poorly ventilated kitchens. Grilled slices of beef, chicken, and lamb slathered in kankankan (see page 32) are served on a stick or sandwiched between baguette bread. Every country makes its spice mixture slightly differently, but it's usually composed of ground ginger, selim pepper (a musky, flavorful spice also known as grains of selim and other names), dried chili powder, peanut flour, and sometimes some dry corn flour.

THE SUYA-CART GUY

If you see a man hauling a motorless rickshaw cart that is emitting the irresistible scent of grilled meat on the busy city streets of a West African metropolis, chances are you've spotted the suya cart guy, on the prowl for hungry patrons. Menus at suya carts are usually nonexistent because the offering always consists of only one item: grilled suya. The thinly sliced pieces of meat are rubbed with the nutty spice blend kankankan and sit at room temperature on large platters, where they tenderize and soak in the flavor of the spices. The simple "kitchen" consists of a large grilling rack placed atop a burning charcoal flame sitting in a low brick structure about six feet wide. The sultry fragrances fill the air as soon as the cooking begins. The hardworking chef-slash-driver covers the rack with the marinated lamb slices on skewers and deftly flips the skewers with

a long pair of tongs as they cook. From time to time, he dips a paintbrush into a recycled tomato can filled with kankankan-infused oil and brushes the glaze over the flaming meat. When the skewers are finished, he hands you his masterpiece on kraft paper with some extra kankankan for dipping and a few slices of raw onion.

THE DIBITERIE IS THE PLACE TO BE

Imagine raucous, jovial patrons discussing politics, soccer games, and wrestling matches over plates of freshly cooked meat wrapped in kraft paper. At a dibiterie, everything is cooked in a large built-in earthen oven, fueled with ardent flames of burning wood. Unlike the suya joints and carts, a dibiterie could offer a wider range of meats: chunky pieces of lamb and goat ribs, legs or other bone-in meat, and offal—heart, gizzards, liver, tripe, the works. I once had a "dibi" (the common name for anything cooked in a dibiterie) of fresh, gamy antelope meat, hunted by the owner himself. Depending on the cut of meat, the pitmaster places the meat closer or farther from the wood fire. Sometimes the meats are wrapped with thick onion slices inside a kraft paper envelope, folded shut, then slow steamed in the back of the oven, where the heat is less intense. Unwrapping the steam-puffed package releases the most amazing aroma of cooked meat, onions, and spices. A typical dibiterie table holds a jar of Dijon mustard, a bottle of Arome Maggi (a popular seasoning), and kani sauce (see page 59). Utensils are available but optional—we believe that food tastes better when eaten by hand. Every dibiterie pitmaster has their own secret marinade. Dibi meat is always prepared from scratch and sold by the kilo or half kilo only.

EID, BARBECUE AS PEACEKEEPER

During Eid al-Fitr, a Muslim holiday also known as the Feast of the Lamb, Senegal and the rest of the Islamic diaspora are filled with the amazingly smoky, sultry scent of lamb parts grilled on an open-air fourneau. As the biblical story goes, Abraham was told to slaughter his son to show his allegiance to God. As he was about

to do it, a lamb appeared, offering its body as sacrifice. (This is where the term *sacrificial lamb* comes from.) This is why every year during Eid, many Muslim households slaughter a lamb. Senegal is a majority Muslim country, so you can imagine how strong the fragrant wafts of lamb grilling on fourneaus are across the land. And to keep with the sense of peacemaking and shared sacrifice, parts of that meat are shared with Christian friends and neighbors: outdoor grilling, sharing meat across religious divides, a communal sense of spirited giving. It doesn't get much better than that.

The combination of my West African roots and my current life in America means that for me, barbecue has been and always will be a versatile and beautiful part of my life that is both a practical everyday cooking technique and a social affair with friends and family. Next time you go to a barbecue, remember that this is not just a singular moment in your backyard. All over the world, people are grilling and partaking in communal meals just as you are. Generously sharing meals is one of the best ways to connect with other people. This is the spirit of teranga in action.

CHICKEN SUYA, YAKITORI-STYLE

SERVES 6 ΛΛΛΛΛΛ

In Lisa's hometown of Tokyo, you can't walk two city blocks without encountering an alluring fabric-laden doorway inviting you in for yakitori, an eating concept based around consuming every single part of the chicken on a skewer. Here, we combine West African flavors with this quintessential Japanese dish by using kankankan and an onion garnish. This recipe calls for boneless chicken thighs, but if you're feeling adventurous or want to really honor the philosophy of using all the parts of the animal, you can also grill savory cuts like liver, gizzard, and heart—just remember to adjust the cook times accordingly.

1 pound boneless chicken thighs (skin-on preferred, but skinless will work)

1 cup Homemade Kankankan (page 32) or store-bought

1 tablespoon vegetable oil

2 garlic cloves, finely chopped

1 teaspoon fine sea salt

½ teaspoon grated fresh ginger

½ cup thinly sliced red onion, for serving

½ cup coarsely chopped roasted peanuts, for serving

Special Equipment: 12 wooden or bamboo skewers (if using wooden skewers, soak them in water for 1 hour before using to prevent them from charring)

Cut the chicken into 1-inch pieces and place them in a shallow dish. Add ½ cup of the kankankan, the oil, garlic, salt, and ginger, and mix well. (Save the other ½ cup kankankan for serving.)

Preheat a barbecue grill, a grill pan, or an oven broiler.

Pierce the chicken pieces with the skewers, 4 or 5 pieces per skewer, and place on the grill or under the broiler until the chicken has some nice charred grill lines and is cooked through, 6 minutes on each side, for a total cook time of 12 minutes. Serve with the remaining kankankan on the side as a dry dip, and sprinkle with red onion slices and chopped peanuts.

PAPA'S FAMOUS CHICKEN YASSA TACOS

SERVES 4 ♈♈♈♈

Bringing a child into the world comes with lots of sleepless nights and beautiful memories of good friends exhibiting immeasurable gestures of kindness. For Lisa and me, one of the happy-memory moments shortly after Naia's birth was when my longtime friend and sous-chef, Papa Mbengue, drove up to our home from his place in Berkeley and brought us a crate full of his delicious chicken yassa tacos. Papa himself is the father of three amazing daughters, and over the years he as worked with me on bringing West African food to special menus at top establishments all over the world, from Barcelona's Cotton House Hotel to Berkeley's esteemed Chez Panisse. Chicken yassa is one of the most popular Senegalese dishes in the diaspora, and here Papa has brought his own vision and creativity to it by combining this simple, bespoke West African flavor with the joy of eating a taco.

2 tablespoons Dijon mustard

2 teaspoons chili powder or cayenne

1 teaspoon ground cumin

1 teaspoon smoked paprika

1 teaspoon chopped fresh thyme

1 garlic clove, minced

1 teaspoon fine sea salt

1 teaspoon freshly ground black pepper

1½ pounds boneless, skinless chicken thighs

1 tablespoon vegetable oil

12 (8-inch) flour tortillas, warmed

1 cup Classic Lemony Yassa Sauce (page 52), for serving

1 avocado, diced, for serving

½ cup chopped fresh cilantro, for serving

1 lime, cut into wedges, for serving

In a small bowl, combine the mustard, chili powder, cumin, paprika, thyme, garlic, salt, and pepper. In a large bowl, rub the chili powder mixture on the chicken to season.

In a large cast-iron skillet, heat the oil over medium-high heat. Working in batches if needed, add the chicken to the skillet in a single layer and cook, turning once, until golden brown and cooked through, 4 to 5 minutes per side. Let cool before cutting it into bite-size pieces. Serve the chicken in tortillas, topped with yassa sauce, avocado, and cilantro, and lime wedges on the side.

SENEGALESE BASSI LAMB STEW AND COUSCOUS

WITH NAVY BEANS PAGE 108

SENEGALESE BASSI LAMB STEW
AND COUSCOUS WITH NAVY BEANS

SERVES 4 TO 6 ♀♀♀♀

In Senegal, we celebrate the Islamic New Year during a festival called Tamkharit. I looked forward to this time of year so much as a child, in part because kids would get dressed up in a fashion reminiscent of Halloween in America, but mostly because we would eat this delicious lamb stew. This is a must-try recipe for all of you who have loved lamb shanks, meat that falls off the bone, or anything prepared in a slow cooker.

BASSI

2 tablespoons vegetable oil

1½ pounds boneless shoulder of mutton, goat, or lamb, cut into 2-inch cubes

1 tablespoon fine sea salt, plus more as needed

1 teaspoon freshly ground black pepper

1 large yellow onion, thinly sliced

1 green bell pepper, chopped

2 tablespoons tomato paste

3 garlic cloves, minced

1 teaspoon ground ginger

2 large carrots, cut into 2-inch chunks

2 sweet potatoes, peeled and cut into 2-inch chunks

1 small cabbage, outer leaves and excess stem removed, cut into 4 or 6 wedges through the core

1 bay leaf

1½ cups fresh cilantro leaves (from 1 small bunch), for serving

COUSCOUS

2 cups regular couscous or dried millet

2 tablespoons extra-virgin olive oil

1 teaspoon fine sea salt

2 cups coarsely chopped pitted dates

1 cup cooked navy beans (canned is okay)

1 cup golden raisins or chopped dried apricot

PREPARE THE BASSI: In a large pot, heat the oil over high heat. Season the meat with the salt and pepper, and cook in batches, turning the meat once, until it turns a lovely golden brown color, about 4 minutes per batch. Set the meat aside in a bowl. Add the onion and bell pepper to the pot over medium-high heat and stir well. Stir in the tomato paste, garlic, and ginger. Cook, stirring regularly so that nothing sticks to the bottom of the pot, until the mixture becomes dark red, about 7 minutes.

Return the meat to the pot. Add 8 cups of water and bring to a boil over high heat. Add the carrots, sweet potato, cabbage, and bay leaf. Cook, stirring occasionally, until the carrots and sweet potatoes are soft and easily pierced with a fork, 20 more minutes. Remove the vegetables using a slotted spoon and set aside in a bowl, loosely covered with an aluminum foil tent to keep them warm. Reduce the heat to medium-low and allow the meat to cook, covered and undisturbed, until soft, about 1 more hour.

Once the meat is ready, return the cooked vegetables to the pot. Before serving, cook until heated through, about 5 minutes. Taste and adjust the seasoning with more salt as needed.

MEANWHILE, PREPARE THE COUSCOUS: In a large heatproof bowl, add the couscous. Bring 4 cups of water to a boil over high heat and carefully pour it over the couscous. Drizzle the oil over the couscous and sprinkle it with the salt. Use a fork to stir the oil and salt to combine with the couscous. Cover the bowl tightly with aluminum foil or reusable plastic wrap and let steam, until the couscous is swollen, fluffy, and soft, about 25 minutes.

Remove the cover and stir the grains with a fork to separate them. Transfer to a platter and add the dates, beans, and raisins. Fold gently to incorporate. Serve with the lamb and lots of sauce, with cilantro sprinkled over.

AUNT MARIE'S SAUCE FEUILLE (LEAFY BEEF STEW)

SERVES 4 TO 6 ꙮꙮꙮꙮ

Lisa's first trip to Dakar was special for many reasons, not least of which was her introduction to my aunt Marie's sauce feuille. This dish is a genuine representation of my roots—generous, heartwarming, and nourishing in all the right ways. It's traditionally made with moringa (read more about this incredible African super ingredient on page 35), cassava or sweet potato leaves, and cabbage. Here, I use collard greens, which are easy to find and still create that homey green color and rich, textured flavor, but if you can source the more traditional cassava leaves, use them!

1½ cups kosher salt, for blanching vegetables

1 small cabbage, cored and thinly sliced, about 4 cups

1 pound collard greens or cassava leaves, stemmed

2 tablespoons peanut or vegetable oil

2 pounds beef shoulder, cut into 2-inch cubes

2 teaspoons fine sea salt, plus more as needed

1 teaspoon freshly ground black pepper

½ cup chopped yellow onion

2 garlic cloves, finely chopped

1 tablespoon grated fresh ginger

¼ cup tomato paste

4 cups chicken stock or water

1 habanero or Scotch bonnet chili, left whole (optional)

Rice or Simply Fonio (page 215), for serving

In a large pot, combine the kosher salt and 1 gallon of water and bring to a boil over high heat. Set a large bowl of ice water alongside. Blanch the cabbage by adding it to the boiling water for 3 minutes, then, using tongs, a slotted spoon, or a strainer, remove the cabbage and transfer it to the ice water to stop the cooking. When cool, drain the cabbage, squeezing out as much water as possible, and set aside. Repeat the blanching process with the collard greens, then finely chop them after draining.

In a Dutch oven or large heavy-bottomed pot, heat the oil over high heat. While the oil is heating, season the beef with 1 teaspoon of the sea salt and ½ teaspoon of the pepper. Add the beef cubes to the pot and cook, stirring so that they brown evenly on all sides, about 5 minutes. Add the onion and sauté until translucent, about 5 more minutes. Add the garlic and ginger, and cook, stirring constantly, until fragrant and with a light golden color, 2 to 3 minutes. Reduce the heat to low, then stir in the tomato paste.

Continue to cook, stirring to make sure the tomato paste doesn't scorch, until the tomato paste turns a dark brick color, 5 more minutes. Add the chicken stock, bring to a boil over high heat, then reduce the heat to low and simmer, partially covered, until the oil rises to the surface, about 15 minutes. Add the remaining 1 teaspoon salt and ½ teaspoon pepper and the habanero (if using). Add the cabbage and collard greens and stir to incorporate, being careful not to burst the habanero while stirring. Simmer until the meat is tender, 40 to 50 more minutes, then taste and adjust the seasoning. Remove the habanero and reserve on the side for those who want the stew extra spicy. Serve warm with rice or fonio.

RICE AND BEEF MBAHAL

SERVES 4 ♈♈♈♈

The original mbahal hails from Gambia and is made with smoked fish and dawadawa (see page 34). It's a classic, somewhat similar to a rice porridge but with a more risotto-like consistency. Over the years, many variations have been created using different meats, some with a smokier or saltier constitution. In my version, I've simplified the recipe so that it can be made with ingredients like fish sauce and tomato paste. What distinguishes this rice dish from the rest is the nuttiness that comes from the peanut flour and the tanginess of the lime and tamarind, which is optional here but highly recommended for its distinct sweet-sour flavor.

2 cups jasmine rice

2 tablespoons peanut or vegetable oil, plus more as needed

2 pounds beef shoulder, cut into 1-inch cubes

2 teaspoons freshly ground black pepper

1 teaspoon fine sea salt

1 cup chopped yellow onion

1 cup cherry tomatoes, halved

1 tablespoon tomato paste

4 cups chicken or beef stock or water

1 medium eggplant, cut into 2-inch cubes (about 3 cups)

2 to 3 tablespoons fish sauce, as needed

2 tablespoons tamarind concentrate (optional)

2 bay leaves

1 habanero or Scotch bonnet chili, left whole

10 medium okra pods, cut into ½-inch slices (optional)

1 cup peanut flour or ½ cup unsweetened creamy peanut butter

1 cup canned black-eyed peas, rinsed and drained

Lime wedges, for serving

½ cup Sauce Dah (page 43), for serving (optional)

In a medium bowl, rinse and drain the rice, then soak it in enough water to cover for 30 minutes.

Meanwhile, in a large pot, heat the oil over medium-high heat. Season the meat with the pepper and salt and add to the hot pot, a few pieces at a time (being careful not to overcrowd). Brown on all sides, stirring occasionally, about 5 minutes per batch. Add more oil if necessary between batches. Stir in the onion and cook until beginning to soften, 2 to 3 minutes. Add the cherry tomatoes and tomato paste, then reduce the heat to low. Cook, stirring from time to time, until the tomatoes break down, about 5 minutes. Add the chicken stock.

Raise the heat to high and return to a boil. Add the eggplant, fish sauce, tamarind (if using), bay leaves, and habanero. Reduce the heat to low and simmer until the eggplant softens, 10 more minutes. Add the okra (if using) and continue cooking until it's tender but still firm to the bite, about 5 more minutes.

Using a slotted spoon, remove the eggplant, habanero, and okra, transfer to a plate, then cover loosely with aluminum foil to keep them warm. Add the peanut flour to the meat broth and stir well to avoid forming clumps.

Drain the rice, then add it to the pot. Cover and simmer over low heat, undisturbed, until the rice is cooked through, 20 to 25 minutes. (The rice should have the consistency of risotto.) Fold in the black-eyed peas. Transfer the rice mixture to a serving platter, then top with the reserved okra, eggplant, and habanero. Serve with lime wedges and sauce dah on the side (if using).

KARAAGE-
STYLE

WEST
AFRICAN FRIED
CHICKEN

KARAAGE-STYLE WEST AFRICAN FRIED CHICKEN

Karaage (pronounced KA-ra-AH-gay) is the Japanese name for fried chicken, another one of those delightful foods that almost every culture enjoys but Lisa's home country does particularly well. The tricks to getting this recipe right are (1) using the Japanese method of thinly coating the chicken with potato starch instead of flour, which makes for a crispier fry, and (2) peanut oil, which both Africans and the Japanese have long used to get that flaky-light texture that keeps you going back for just one more piece. (If you're allergic to peanuts, try another light vegetable oil, like sunflower oil.) I also add mustard to the marinade to give it a slightly tangy twist and serve it with moyo sauce.

MARINADE

1 tablespoon grated onion

2 garlic cloves, finely minced

1 tablespoon fresh lemon juice

1 tablespoon grated fresh ginger

1 tablespoon Dijon mustard (optional)

CHICKEN

6 boneless, skinless chicken thighs, cut into 2-inch chunks (about 1½ pounds)

1 cup potato starch

1 teaspoon fine sea salt

1 teaspoon freshly ground black pepper

Peanut oil, for frying

Lemon wedges, for serving

Moyo Sauce Goes with Everything (page 56), for serving

PREPARE THE MARINADE: In a shallow dish, combine the onion, garlic, lemon juice, ginger, and mustard (if using).

PREPARE THE CHICKEN: Add the chicken to the marinade and toss until each piece is completely coated. Cover with plastic wrap and refrigerate overnight.

The next day, in a large bowl, combine the potato starch, salt, and pepper. Remove the chicken pieces, one by one, from the marinade and roll each piece in the potato starch mixture until completely coated. Shake off any excess potato starch mixture, then place on a plate.

Line a platter or sheet pan with paper towels and set aside.

In a large heavy-bottomed pot or deep skillet, add enough oil so that it goes about 3 inches up the sides. Heat the oil over medium-high heat until it reaches about 350°F, using the Ginger Oil Testing Method (see page 79), if convenient. Using a pair of tongs, remove the coated chicken pieces one by one from the plate and place them in the oil to fry in small batches, making sure not to overcrowd the pot. Fry the chicken pieces until they are a light golden color, turning once with a pair of tongs to make sure that they are evenly fried on all sides, about 3 minutes. With your tongs, transfer the fried pieces to the paper towel–lined platter and allow them to cool while you repeat with the remaining batches.

When all the chicken has been fried once, raise the oil temperature to 375°F (use the same oil-testing trick on page 79, this time looking for a more vigorous bubbling). Fry the chicken again until the crust becomes a lovely golden brown color, about 1 more minute. Drain the chicken on a new set of paper towels. Serve hot or at room temperature with lemon wedges and moyo sauce on the side.

BIG BOSS'S CHICKEN
(AKA POULET DG)

SERVES 4 ♈♈♈♈

Big Boss's chicken represents the perfect balance of power and humor, West African–style. DG is an acronym for "directeur general"—which means CEO in French. This dish, often found in Cameroon or Côte d'Ivoire, has some similarities with the classic French poulet fricassée in that it is a chicken and vegetable stew, but instead of being drenched in cream, it's cooked gently with ginger, plantains, and tomatoes. The uncompromised juiciness of the chicken thighs, the kick of intensity from the ginger, and the occasional sweetness of the plantains make this unforgettable dish a delight no matter where you stand on the ladder of authority.

6 bone-in chicken thighs (about 2 pounds), skin on or off, or 1 whole chicken (about 3 pounds), cut into 8 parts

2 tablespoons extra-virgin olive oil

6 garlic cloves, finely chopped

2 teaspoons chopped fresh thyme

2 teaspoons fine sea salt, plus more as needed

½ teaspoon freshly ground black pepper

4 large, firm plantains (not overly ripe)

Peanut or sunflower oil, for frying

1 cup chopped yellow onion

½ cup chopped green bell pepper

½ cup chopped red bell pepper

1 tablespoon coarsely chopped fresh ginger

8 plum tomatoes, coarsely chopped

½ cup chicken stock or water

1 large carrot, sliced into ¼-inch-thick rounds

1 handful of green beans, trimmed and cut into 1-inch pieces

2 tablespoons Nokos Seasoning (page 33; optional)

1 small bunch of fresh cilantro, coarsely chopped, for serving

In a large bowl, add the chicken and season with the olive oil, half the garlic, the thyme, salt, and pepper. Cover and marinate for 30 minutes at room temperature, or at least 2 hours and up to overnight in the refrigerator.

Meanwhile, peel the plantains and cut them into 1-inch-thick rounds. In a medium saucepan, add

enough peanut oil so it goes about 2 inches up the sides. Heat the oil over medium-high heat. Add the plantain slices and fry until golden brown on both sides, 1 to 2 minutes per side. Remove the plantains from the pan, then remove the pan from the heat to allow the oil to cool slightly. (Do not discard the oil.)

(RECIPE CONTINUES)

Preheat the oven broiler to high.

Line up the chicken on a sheet pan, skin-side up, and place under the broiler, ideally 5 to 6 inches from the heat source. (If you don't have a broiler, use an oven preheated to 500°F.) Broil, adjusting the pan as needed for even browning, until the skin is deeply browned, crispy, and charred in spots, 10 to 15 minutes. Using a pair of tongs, flip the chicken and continue to cook under the broiler until browned and charred in spots, about 10 more minutes. Remove the sheet pan from the broiler and let it sit at room temperature.

In a Dutch oven or large heavy-bottomed pot, heat 2 tablespoons of the oil used for frying the plantains over medium heat. Add the onion and stir until soft and translucent, about 5 minutes. Add the green and red bell peppers, the ginger, and the remaining garlic, and cook, stirring continuously, until fragrant and the onion is a slightly golden brown color, about 3 more minutes. Add the tomatoes, raise the heat to high, and cook, stirring occasionally to avoid scorching, until the tomatoes begin to release their juices, about 3 minutes. Add the chicken stock, allow the mixture to come to a boil, then add the carrots and chicken, along with the juice that has accumulated in the pan. Reduce the heat to medium-low, then cover and simmer until the carrots are soft and the chicken is tender and cooked, about 15 more minutes. Add the green beans and nokos (if using), and cook until the beans are tender, about 5 minutes. Taste and adjust the seasoning with more salt as needed. Add the fried plantains and gently fold them into the stew. Transfer to a large platter and top with the cilantro. Serve immediately.

BOOZY PAIRINGS FOR YOUR AFRICAN MEAL

Almost as important as cooking the right food is pairing it with the right beverages. While cocktails are fun to make, I'm going to go out on a limb and say that nothing pairs better with the rich, hearty dishes in this book and the intense spices and flavors of West African cuisine than a good old beer. Brands like La Gazelle, Flag Spéciale, and Castel are popular in West Africa, but any blond or lager beer from your local grocery or liquor store is sure to be a great complement to our food. (Guinness, the globally renowned Irish stout, is hugely popular in Nigeria, though I never really understood why.) If you're looking for a healthier and lighter option, you might enjoy the fonio beer brewed by my friend Garrett Oliver from Brooklyn Brewery.

Wait, what is this you're saying? You're not a beer drinker? No problem! A good wine will elevate the experience of eating West African food at home, making it a slightly more buttoned-up affair. For recipes that use chilies like Scotch bonnet or West African Piri-Piri Sauce (page 58), you might consider an easy, fruity, light-bodied wine to balance out the heat from the spices, like a chenin blanc from South Africa. Heartier meat dishes and stews might benefit from a pairing with a full-bodied red like pinot noir or burgundy, whose higher acidity levels will cut through the richness of ingredients like red palm oil. Light white wines, like a Riesling or a Sancerre, work perfectly with the fish and seafood recipes in this book. And, of course, let's not forget that a little bit of sparkly is always a good option for any occasion.

DINNER PARTIES, WEST AFRICAN-STYLE

America has an unwieldy and emotionally complex dinner party culture. Evening gatherings are common in West Africa, too, but in parts of the United States, what type of dinner party you throw is like a plexiglass display case for your inner and outer identity. I've noticed how some people in this country fret for hours over things like lighting, the space between cutlery, the ratio of size of placemat to size of plate to size of portion of food, the color of the napkins, seating arrangements, what they wear in their own home when folks come over. And then they talk about the dinner party so-and-so threw for years to follow. What you serve at these highly personalized, curiously scrutinized dinner parties often seems like a very big deal.

It's wonderful! But also, aspiring to this level of perfection in hosting can be nerve-racking, and I imagine this is part of the reason why cookbooks are so popular.

A West African dinner party can be anything you want. It can be meticulously planned and sophisticated, or it can be two people eating off paper plates and having an intimate moment together, where nobody is watching. Some of the best dinner parties I've hosted have been just Lisa and I at our home in Northern California, gazing at the sunset and recollecting the highlights of our day. It can be a holiday party packed with friends and family, with shared pots and plates, conversation, and laughter, hands reaching in every direction. It can be just you and a glass of wine, enjoying your own beautiful company because you deserve a quiet night alone when you don't have to take care of anyone but yourself. It can be a celebration of the end of a season, or a milestone, or a cultural tradition—customized to fit who you are and what type of mood you're in. And some more good news: All the pressure is off! Perfection is not a prerequisite. We love colorful, mismatched fabrics, food that's plopped generously onto large shareable plates. As long as you have the right spirit, you can manifest a wonderful West African–style gathering without overthinking it. All you really need is an adventurous spirit and some good vibes to pair with the food you will cook—with this book as your guide.

For Lisa's birthday last year, we invited a half dozen friends over to our home and had family-style platters filled with Blackened Salmon with Moyo Sauce (page 138), Baked Ginger-Chili Plantain Kelewele (page 179), an array of colorful roasted fall vegetables, a side of string beans, and some curried fonio (see page 31). It was the perfect array of flavors, colors, and textures to celebrate another trip around the sun for Lisa, and the gradual shift we were all feeling from fall to winter. By contrast, for Naia's birthday, which is in the middle of summer, we had about twenty people over, and I prepared small plates full of grilled corn, chopped fresh cilantro, Casamance Green Mango Salsa (page 53), and grilled beef and chicken and tofu, alongside some store-bought corn tortillas, for a DIY African-inspired taco party. It was simple, abundant, delicious, and a big hit with adults and kids alike.

Even though neither Lisa nor I is originally from the United States, we've come to love the American rituals of festive dining, and are always finding ways to celebrate life over generous servings of delicious food.

ROASTED PIRI-PIRI CHICKEN

SERVES 4 ♈♈♈♈

This deliciously spiced chicken dish from Angola and Mozambique very simply combines piri-piri sauce with a spatchcocked chicken. Spatchcocking—removing the backbone of the bird so that it can lie flat on the cooking surface—might seem daunting, but it's an incredibly useful kitchen trick. Also known as butterflying, this technique reduces cook time and increases the direct exposure of the meat to the heat, resulting in a barbecue-like taste and texture. The chicken needs to marinate for at least four hours before being cooked, so if you're making this dish for dinner—which you most definitely should!—be sure you plan ahead.

½ cup plus 2 tablespoons West African Piri-Piri Sauce (page 58)

¼ cup extra-virgin olive oil

¼ cup fresh lemon juice

1 teaspoon fine sea salt

1 teaspoon freshly ground black pepper

1 whole chicken (about 4 pounds), spatchcocked

In a medium bowl, add ½ cup of the piri-piri sauce, the oil, lemon juice, salt, and pepper, and whisk to combine. Pour half of the piri-piri mixture into a baking dish large enough to hold the flattened chicken. Place the chicken in the baking dish, skin-side up, open wide with wings tipped under the breasts. Pour the remaining piri-piri mixture over the top. Cover and marinate in the refrigerator for at least 4 hours or overnight.

Preheat the oven to 400°F.

Remove the chicken from the marinade and arrange, skin-side up, on a large sheet pan or in a cast-iron skillet. Discard the remaining marinade. Place the chicken in the oven and roast until the skin is browned and an instant-read thermometer inserted into the thickest part of the thigh registers 165°F, 50 minutes to 1 hour. Remove the chicken from the oven, cover lightly with aluminum foil, allow it to rest for about 10 minutes, then transfer it to a serving platter. Pour the pan drippings into a heatproof bowl and stir in the remaining 2 tablespoons piri-piri sauce. Brush over the chicken just before serving.

POULET BRAISÉ,
OR IVORIAN ROASTED CHICKEN

SERVES 4 TO 6 АААА

There are many beautiful places to visit in Côte d'Ivoire, but my favorite venues are the easy open-air markets called allocodromes, where you can get delicious meats like this roasted chicken dish for extremely reasonable prices. The combination of flavors in poulet braisé is complex without being overly complicated, with bursts of heat and flavor with every bite. If you're a hot-chicken-wing-loving type of person, I have a feeling this might just become your new favorite dish. Serve with Mashed Sweet Plantains (page 202), a fresh salad, and some rice—and you have yourself a full-course Ivorian feast!

MARINADE

¼ cup Dijon mustard

¼ cup garlic cloves, smashed with the side of a knife

Juice of 1 lime

1 habanero or Scotch bonnet chili, seeded and finely chopped

1 tablespoon grated fresh ginger

1 tablespoon vegetable oil, plus more as needed

1 teaspoon fine sea salt

½ teaspoon freshly ground black pepper

½ teaspoon smoked paprika

1 whole chicken (4 to 5 pounds), spatchcocked or cut into 6 or 8 pieces

Moyo Sauce Goes with Everything (page 56), for serving

PREPARE THE MARINADE: In a blender or food processor, combine the mustard, garlic, lime juice, habanero, ginger, oil, salt, pepper, and paprika, and purée until smooth, adding more oil as needed to facilitate blending.

Place the chicken on a clean work surface. Using a sharp knife, make slits in the chicken skin to ensure the marinade seeps through and rub the skin with the marinade. Let sit in a large bowl, covered with plastic wrap, for 30 minutes at room temperature or refrigerate for 2 hours or up to overnight.

Preheat the oven to 500°F.

If the chicken was marinated overnight, remove it from the refrigerator and allow to come to room temperature before cooking. Place the chicken on a sheet pan or other ovenproof pan and place in the oven. Cook the chicken until the juices run clear and the skin is blistering and dark, about 40 minutes. (If you have an instant-read thermometer, the temperature of the legs should be 165° to 170°F.) Remove the chicken from the oven, transfer it to a platter, and allow it to sit, loosely covered with aluminum foil, for about 10 minutes. Serve hot with moyo sauce on the side.

THIEBOU YAPP,
THE ULTIMATE RICE PILAF

SERVES 4 ⋏⋏⋏⋏

If you love paella or biryani or, for that matter, if you simply love when rice and meat live in perfect harmony in one happy dish, then it's very likely that you will also love this favorite Senegalese dish that combines aromatic jasmine rice with lamb seasoned with savory nokos. Like its Spanish counterpart, thiebou yapp is best served on a big round platter so that everyone can enjoy it at the same time. For maximum effect, I highly recommend topping this off with mustard-onion relish. In Senegal, you often see this dish decorated with boiled eggs placed around the bowl.

NOTE: To make soft-boiled eggs: In a small saucepan, add about 1 inch of water, cover with a lid, and bring to a boil over medium-high heat. Carefully add the eggs, cover again, and boil for 7 to 8 minutes (depending on how soft you want the yolk to be). Remove the eggs and run under cold water until they are cool enough to handle.

2 pounds boneless lamb shoulder, cut into 2-inch cubes

2 teaspoons fine sea salt, plus more as needed

1 teaspoon freshly ground black pepper

½ cup peanut or vegetable oil

1 cup finely chopped yellow onion

¼ cup Nokos Seasoning (page 33)

2 bay leaves

2 medium carrots, diced into ½-inch cubes

2 cups jasmine rice, rinsed and drained

½ cup frozen peas (not thawed)

Mustard-Onion Relish (page 47), for serving (optional)

2 medium soft-boiled eggs, peeled and halved (see Note), for serving (optional)

Pat the lamb dry with paper towels, season with the salt and pepper, then set aside.

In a Dutch oven or large heavy-bottomed pot, heat the oil over high heat. Working in batches, add the lamb and sauté, stirring only occasionally to allow the meat to evenly brown, about 8 minutes. After the last batch, return all the lamb to the pot. Reduce the heat to medium, add the onion, and continue to cook, stirring constantly, until the onion is soft and lightly browned,

another 4 minutes. Add 2 tablespoons of the nokos and stir to coat the meat, about 1 minute. Add 3 cups of water and the bay leaves to the pot. Bring to a boil over high heat, reduce the heat to medium-low, cover, and simmer, undisturbed, until the meat is tender, about 45 minutes. Taste and adjust the seasoning, adding more salt as needed, then stir in the remaining 2 tablespoons nokos and the carrots.

Add the rice to the pot and stir once to combine all the ingredients. Raise the heat to high and bring to a boil. Reduce the heat to low, cover tightly, and cook until the liquid is absorbed and the rice is soft to the bite, about 15 minutes. Add the frozen peas to the pot, mix thoroughly, cover again, and cook for another 5 minutes. Serve hot, with mustard-onion relish and soft-boiled eggs (if using).

MAMAN'S CRISPY HERB-CRUSTED CHICKEN

SERVES 4 ♁♁♁♁

One of the things I miss the most from my home country is my mom's cooking. She had a philosophy when it came to the food she made for our family and everybody else who chanced upon our meal table: flavors first! This chicken recipe is inspired by the way my mom marinated her chicken, with a mélange of delicious spices like rosemary, thyme, parsley, and pepper. True to her style, it is full of flavor—and love. This recipe is here in her memory, and I hope it makes its way to your table soon, too.

8 bone-in, skin-on chicken thighs (about 3 pounds)

3 garlic cloves

1 tablespoon fine sea salt

¼ cup extra-virgin olive oil

2 tablespoons chopped fresh flat-leaf parsley

1 tablespoon chopped fresh rosemary

1 tablespoon chopped fresh thyme

2 medium yellow onions, cut into 1-inch-thick rounds

1 large lemon, sliced into thin rounds

1 teaspoon freshly ground black pepper

Cooked rice or Mashed Sweet Plantains (page 202), for serving

Rinse the chicken and pat it dry with a paper towel. For each thigh, using a sharp knife, cut 2 or 3 slits about ½ inch deep and 1 inch long across the chicken skin and flesh. Using a mortar and pestle or a small food processor, mash or pulse the garlic and salt into a paste. Then add 2 tablespoons of the oil, the parsley, rosemary, and thyme, and continue mashing or pulsing until combined. Rub the herb mixture into the chicken, making sure to go under the skin and into the slits. Cover with plastic wrap and allow the chicken to marinate at room temperature for 30 minutes, or overnight in the refrigerator. (If refrigerating, make sure to return the chicken to room temperature before starting to cook it.)

Place an oven rack in the middle of the oven. Preheat the oven to 450°F.

Place the onion slices in one layer in the bottom of a large ovenproof dish. Scatter the lemon slices on top of the onions. Place the chicken thighs, skin-side up, on top of the onion and lemon slices. Sprinkle the pepper over the chicken and drizzle the remaining 2 tablespoons oil over the chicken skin. Bake the chicken until it is crisp and has a beautiful golden color on the skin, and the juices are clear, about 40 minutes.

Remove the dish from the oven and transfer the onions, chicken, and lemon to a serving platter. Collect the juices that have pooled at the bottom and pour them into a small saucepan. Spoon off the fat at the surface. Serve the chicken with the pan juices and rice or plantains.

SEAFOOD

JOYFUL FEASTS
FROM THE SEA

JOYFUL FEASTS
FROM THE SEA

SEAFOOD

Lisa and I are from opposite ends of the earth—literally!—but one common thread in the places where we come from and the places we love to spend time in is the ocean. We were both born and raised in big port cities that have been around for a very long time. Lisa grew up in Tokyo, moved to California, and spent her summers in Hawaii, so her sacred body of water is the Pacific Ocean. I grew up in Dakar, moved to New York, and have dedicated my life to bringing light to the stories of food making it across the Middle Passage, so my origins are rooted in the Atlantic Ocean. We love the ocean so much that we named our daughter Naia, which means "dolphin" in the Hawaiian language.

Seafood is an integral part of our diet at home. Lisa, Naia, and I eat fish at least once a week, bought fresh from the local farmers' market or fishmonger and prepared with love, West African–style. This chapter is full of flavorful, culturally significant seafood soups and stews. We eat these a lot in our home, perhaps because I'm from the westernmost coast of Africa (Senegal) and now live on the westernmost coast of the United States (California). Here, you'll learn how to make some of our most popular seafood dishes, like the soothing, aromatic Seafood Okra Soupou Kanja (page 137), a stew with scallops and mussels; the limey and flavorful Poached Calamari Caldou in Tomato and Lemon Broth (page 150); and one of my personal favorites, Shrimp and Fonio Grits (page 144).

Every coastal country in the world has fishermen with deep and authentic expertise in their craft, who know their part of the sea like the back of their hand. Fishing techniques like angling, trapping, and netting are literally as old as human civilization itself. Big sea fishermen often work together regardless of where in the world they are from. Their common language is a knowledge and love of the sea. It is in this beautiful, vast, mysterious space that we, over centuries and across geographies, have claimed some of our most audacious culinary experiments.

All the recipes here call for sustainable fish—nothing that is depleting the oceans or challenges the ecosystem in any significant way. In our current world, we've forgotten a lot of things, like how to take good care of our planet, and how to pay homage to our ancestors and the original occupants of our lands and waters. It's important to hold on to our respect for the ocean—its divine nature, its ability to give abundantly, and its endless beauty and mystery. Many cultures worship the sea and have water deities to prove it. Poseidon is the god of the sea in ancient Greek religion and myth, and in Hawaii, Kanaloa is the god of the sea. Mami Wata, a mythical water spirit, is revered and feared across the African continent. Honoring the ocean is an important part of how we must live today and what we can leave behind for our kids, so that they have a balanced ecosystem to live in—and nutritious, tasty seafood to eat.

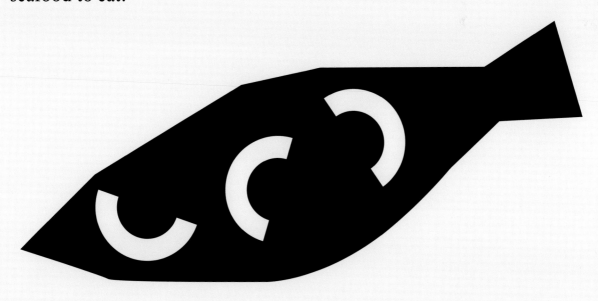

SEAFOOD OKRA SOUPOU KANJA

SERVES 4 TO 6 ♟♟♟♟

The name soupou kanja may not ring a bell, but you've likely heard of gumbo, a mainstay of New Orleans cuisine. Soupou kanja is the origin of that Creole seafood stew. Here, I offer a twist on the classic African version, using scallops and mussels instead of shrimp and sausage, which gives it a freshness and elegance reminiscent of the atmosphere of my ocean-side hometown of Dakar. For a slightly smokier flavor, take the option of adding some mackerel, which you can buy in a can or at your local fish market.

1 cup bottled clam juice

1 cup finely chopped yellow onion

2 cups crushed tomatoes (about half of a 28-ounce can)

1 tablespoon fish sauce

1 Scotch bonnet or habanero chili, left whole (optional)

1 smoked mackerel, skin off, bones removed, and cut into 1-inch cubes, or about 1 cup canned (optional)

1 teaspoon fine sea salt

1 pound large sea scallops (about 12)

1 pound fresh or frozen half-shell New Zealand mussels

20 to 24 okra pods, as needed, cut into ¼-inch slices

¼ cup sustainably sourced red palm oil (see page 31)

Cooked rice, Simply Fonio (page 215), or Fufu (page 228), for serving

In a large pot, combine 1 cup of water, the clam juice, and onion. Bring to a boil over medium-high heat, then reduce the heat to medium-low. Cook until the onion is softened, 5 to 7 minutes. Stir in the tomatoes, fish sauce, and Scotch bonnet (if using). Return the heat to medium-high, bring to a boil, and boil for about 2 minutes. Reduce the heat to medium-low and continue to cook until the sauce thickens, about 10 minutes. Stir in the smoked mackerel (if using) and salt. Stir with a wooden spoon to incorporate, being careful not to crush the Scotch bonnet.

Raise the heat to medium-high and cook until the broth begins to boil. Add the scallops, mussels, okra, and oil, and stir to incorporate. Cook until the scallops are opaque and starting to slightly break apart at the edges and the okra is still green, about 5 minutes. Serve with the rice or another starch of your choice.

BLACKENED SALMON
WITH MOYO SAUCE

SERVES 4 ᚛᚛᚛᚛

Salmon is one of the most nutritious, versatile fish in the sea. The key to making perfect salmon is to find a center cut—the thicker the better—and cook it in a cast-iron skillet, which conducts heat well and therefore allows the surface of the salmon to sear and blacken quickly without overcooking the whole fish. Always preheat your cast-iron skillet until it's very hot before adding the salmon, and avoid crowding the skillet with too many fillets at once. The fish should sit comfortably in the skillet, with plenty of room around it.

SPICE BLEND

2 tablespoons smoked paprika

1 tablespoon cayenne pepper

1 tablespoon onion powder

2 teaspoons fine sea salt

½ teaspoon freshly ground black pepper

¼ teaspoon dried thyme

¼ teaspoon dried basil

¼ teaspoon dried oregano

4 (6-ounce) skin-on salmon fillets

¼ cup extra-virgin olive oil

Moyo Sauce Goes with Everything (page 56), for serving

Cooked rice or atieke (see page 35), for serving

PREPARE THE SPICE BLEND: In a small bowl, combine the paprika, cayenne, onion powder, salt, pepper, thyme, basil, and oregano, and mix well.

Brush each salmon fillet on both sides with approximately 1 teaspoon of the oil, then sprinkle the spice blend evenly over both sides of each fillet.

In a large, heavy cast-iron skillet, heat 2 tablespoons of the oil over high heat. Add the salmon, flesh-side down, and cook until blackened, 2 to 3 minutes, without disturbing the fish (be sure to have your windows open and your exhaust fan on in case it gets smoky). Using a spatula or a pair of tongs, carefully flip the fillets. Reduce the heat to medium and continue cooking until the skin is crisp and blackened and the flesh is easily flaked with a fork, 5 to 6 more minutes (depending on the thickness of the fillets). Serve hot, topped with moyo sauce, and with the rice or starch of your choice on the side.

HERB-ROASTED HALIBUT CHERMOULA

SERVES 4 ∧∧∧∧

Chermoula, a North African–inspired marinade made with spices, herbs, lemon, and olive oil, is an all-time favorite at my restaurant in New York City. At Teranga, I serve it with salmon, but here I use halibut because it's a simple whitefish that's easy to roast, has a satisfying firmness, and goes so well with the chermoula sauce. (If you feel like having salmon instead, it is a most welcome substitute.)

1 cup extra-virgin olive oil

½ cup packed coarsely chopped fresh flat-leaf parsley

½ cup packed coarsely chopped fresh cilantro

2 scallions, finely chopped

2 garlic cloves, minced

2 tablespoons fresh lemon juice

1 teaspoon ground cumin

1 teaspoon fine sea salt, plus more as needed

½ teaspoon smoked paprika

Large pinch of crushed red pepper flakes, plus more as needed

4 halibut fillets, skin off (about 2 pounds)

1 small lemon, thinly sliced

Preheat the oven to 450°F.

In a blender or small food processor, combine the oil, parsley, cilantro, scallions, garlic, lemon juice, cumin, salt, paprika, and red pepper flakes. Mix until a little chunky and not uniformly smooth. Set aside. (You can make the chermoula in advance and keep it in a resealable jar with a tight-fitting lid for up to 2 weeks in the fridge.)

Place the fillets in a broiler-safe dish and brush each of the fillets with about 2 tablespoons of the herb mixture. Top the fillets with several slices of lemon. Bake until the fillets start to turn opaque, about 10 minutes.

Preheat the oven broiler to high.

Transfer the baking dish to the broiler to brown the tops of the fillets, 1 to 2 minutes. Sprinkle with more salt and red pepper flakes as needed. Serve hot.

PAIN BOULETTE
(SENEGALESE FISH SANDWICH)

MAKES 4 SANDWICHES (OR 14 TO 16 BALLS)

Since Dakar is a port town, fish is everywhere, and due to our French colonial history, piles of baguettes line the corner stores throughout the city—it's easy to see why this saucy fish sandwich is so popular. There's a funny, campy song somewhere in the annals of Senegalese music history dedicated entirely to this sandwich, which is lovingly called pain boulette at home. The backstory of the song is a wonderful snapshot of that particular moment in time, during the 1970s, in that particular corner of the earth. James Brown's funky beats were making waves in Senegal, but people weren't quite sure what the lyrics were saying, so someone rewrote them to be about making sandwiches out of fish balls and stale bread when you don't have money for anything else!

1 pound skinless cod or other flaky whitefish fillet, cut into 1-inch pieces

½ cup finely crushed stale bread or bread crumbs

2 garlic cloves, minced

1 tablespoon chopped fresh flat-leaf parsley

¾ teaspoon cayenne pepper

½ teaspoon fine sea salt

¼ teaspoon freshly ground black pepper

½ cup all-purpose flour

¼ cup vegetable oil

2 cups West African Red Sauce (page 51)

1 baguette, cut into 4 pieces

In a blender or food processor, add the cod, bread, garlic, parsley, cayenne, salt, and pepper. Process on medium-high until a thick dough forms. Using your hands, shape the dough into balls that are about 1 inch in diameter (14 to 16 balls). In a shallow bowl, add the flour, lightly dredge the fish balls in the flour, and transfer to a plate. Refrigerate until they become firm to the touch, about 30 minutes.

Line a plate with paper towels and set aside.

In a large heavy-bottomed skillet, heat the oil over medium-high heat. Using your hands or a spoon, carefully add the fish balls to the pan and cook, turning frequently, until nicely browned on all sides, about 10 minutes. Remove from the heat and transfer the fish balls with a slotted spoon to the paper towel–lined plate to absorb the extra oil. Pour out the remaining oil and wipe out the pan. Use the same pan to heat the red sauce over medium heat. Once the sauce is hot, return the fish balls to the sauce. Divide the balls among the pieces of baguette and serve warm.

SHRIMP AND FONIO GRITS

SERVES 4 ⚐⚐⚐⚐

There is a long and resilient history of call and response in African cultures, an often-improvisational, ongoing conversation through music, dance, and religious rituals, in which one person or group presents the other with something to respond to. Think of a reverend in a Black church, or a drumming circle, or a jazz band. It connects people to one another and to the earth. It roots us in our legacy and makes us more present. It's the rhythm that beats in our souls and makes us want to dance!

Many of the recipes in this book are traditional West African menu items that have been adapted for the Western world. This one is a little bit different. Shrimp and grits have long been a favorite in American Southern cuisine. Many people attribute the dish's origins to captive Africans in South Carolina, and some have traced it back farther to Mozambique. The exchange of food wisdom, like song and dance, is a call and response. This is my response to the call of Southern shrimp and grits. Instead of the usual corn grits, I use the ancient African grain fonio, which is lighter and easier on the gut.

1 pound large shrimp, peeled and deveined

3 garlic cloves, minced

2 teaspoons fine sea salt

1 teaspoon freshly ground black pepper

1 teaspoon smoked paprika

¼ teaspoon cayenne pepper

2 cups chicken stock or water

2 cups whole milk

6 tablespoons (¾ stick) unsalted butter, cubed, or extra-virgin olive oil

1 cup fonio (see page 215)

1 cup grated Cheddar cheese

2 tablespoons vegetable oil

2 scallions, thinly sliced, for serving

In a medium bowl, combine the shrimp, garlic, 1 teaspoon of the salt, ½ teaspoon of the pepper, the paprika, and cayenne. Marinate in the refrigerator while you prepare the fonio.

In a large saucepan, combine the chicken stock, milk, butter, the remaining 1 teaspoon salt, and the remaining ½ teaspoon pepper, and bring to a boil over high heat. Slowly stir in the fonio. Return to a boil, then reduce the heat to its lowest setting, cover tightly, and cook until thickened, 10 minutes. Uncover and fold in the cheese with a wooden spoon until melted. Remove the pot from the heat and cover the pot to keep the fonio warm while you cook the shrimp.

In a large heavy-bottomed skillet, heat the oil over medium-high heat. Add the marinated shrimp and sauté until they turn pink, 1 to 2 minutes per side. Divide the fonio among 4 plates, place the shrimp on top, and sprinkle with the scallions. Serve immediately.

SMOKED FISH AND RAINBOW CHARD KONTOMIRE STEW

SERVES 4 TO 6 ⅍⅍⅍⅍

You know what I love about stews from the motherland? In addition to being hearty and tasty, they are often incredibly healthy, too. Kontomire is Ghanaian comfort food at its best, but my version substitutes the greens from the traditional cocoyam (an herbaceous root vegetable more commonly known as taro) with rainbow chard, which is easier to find outside of Africa and is an excellent source of vitamins K, A, and C, magnesium, fiber, potassium, and iron. The secret ingredient in this recipe is egusi, which I talk more about on page 35, but if you don't have egusi, you can use pumpkin seeds instead.

1 cup egusi seeds (see page 35) or raw shelled pumpkin seeds

2½ pounds plum tomatoes, coarsely chopped

1 cup chopped yellow onion

3 tablespoons minced fresh ginger

4 garlic cloves, minced

1 habanero or Scotch bonnet chili, seeded and minced

½ cup sustainably sourced red palm oil (see page 31) or vegetable oil

1 tablespoon tomato paste

2 cups coarsely chopped smoked mackerel or smoked herring (skin off and bones removed)

2 teaspoons fine sea salt, plus more as needed

1 pound rainbow chard, stemmed and leaves cut into thin strips

Fufu (page 228), Mashed Sweet Plantains (page 202), or cooked rice, for serving

In a blender or food processor, add the egusi seeds and pulse to a fine powder. Transfer the powder to a separate bowl and gradually stir in water, 1 tablespoonful at a time, until the consistency reaches a thin paste. Set aside.

Using the same blender, add the tomatoes, ½ cup of the onion, the ginger, garlic, and habanero, and pulse on the low-medium setting until coarsely chopped. Transfer to a medium bowl and set aside.

In a large pot, heat the oil over medium heat until it begins to smoke. Add the remaining ½ cup onion and stir occasionally with a wooden spoon until browned, about 10 minutes. Add the tomato paste to the pot with the onion and stir continuously until the tomato paste darkens to a deep red color, about 3 minutes. Add the tomato mixture to the pot and stir. Reduce the heat to low, then allow the mixture to simmer, partially covered, until it thickens, about 25 minutes. Stir in the smoked mackerel. Add the salt and slowly pour in the egusi paste. Stir to combine, then allow everything to simmer until the egusi is incorporated, another 5 minutes. Add the rainbow chard to the stew, stir to combine, and cook until the strips soften and wilt, about 1 minute. Taste and adjust the seasoning as needed. Serve with the starch of your choice.

SMOKING FISH BY THE BEACH IN SENEGAL

A wonderful thing about fish is that they are so amazing when they are fresh. The shadow side of this is that fresh fish are also highly perishable. This is why the imported fish we get in North America have been frozen at least once. In West Africa, we have another common solution for preservation: smoking. In inland countries like Mali and Burkina Faso, this is the main way that people get their servings of fish. (Smoked fish, like beef jerky, can last forever and therefore does fine on long journeys in hot-temperature zones.)

Smoked fish is also an important and unique flavor agent in West African cuisine. Even in coastal Senegal, where fresh seafood is abundant, we still love to smoke our fish and use it as a seasoning or to supplement sauces and stews as an ingredient. The most commonly smoked fish are often also the boniest ones, like sardines and anchovies. Historically, these little guys are the least popular at the market, so instead of taking them straight to the fish market, the fishermen's wives would smoke them, remove as many of the bones as they could, and add the flesh to their cooking as a smoky flavor agent.

On "smoking" days in fishing villages that span many miles across the West African coastline, piles of fish covered with coarse sea salt are placed on metal grates sitting atop low brick structures with burning millet straws underneath. The rising gray plumes can be seen from miles away. On these days, the smell of smoked fish envelops the land.

When making recipes that call for dried, smoked fish at home, chances are you can still find some amazing options near you. Smoked boneless whitefish like sable, cod, herring, and sardines are often sold next to fresh fish by fishmongers at your local market. You can even find canned smoked sardines and anchovies online. (Make sure you use the dried varieties, not the wet, canned type.)

POACHED CALAMARI CALDOU IN TOMATO AND LEMON BROTH

SERVES 4 ♀♀♀♀

When I was growing up in Dakar, every kid on the block was known for the food their mom was best at making. Benjo's mom, who was from Casamance, was famous for her soupou kanja. Our next-door neighbors, the Diallos, always had terrific mafé. My friend Aida's mom, who was from Saint-Louis in the north, prepared the best thieboudienne in the neighborhood. My mom? She was known for her caldou. Light and flavorful, this dish's signature trait is the way the seafood soaks peacefully in a simple, elegant broth. My mom made hers with carp, but I chose calamari because I find the tender bite of the squid to be in perfect harmony with the soupy base.

1 cup chopped plum tomatoes

1 cup chopped yellow onion

1 habanero or Scotch bonnet chili, seeded and chopped (optional)

1 garlic clove, finely chopped

1 tablespoon fish sauce

1 pound whole calamari, cut into ¾-inch rings with tentacles

1 teaspoon fine sea salt, plus more as needed

About 20 young okra pods, trimmed

Juice from 1 large lemon

Cooked rice or Simply Fonio (page 215), for serving

½ cup Sauce Dah (page 43), for serving (optional)

In a large pot, add 4 cups of water, the tomatoes, onion, habanero (if using), garlic, and fish sauce. Bring to a boil over high heat and add the calamari and salt. Return to a boil, then reduce the heat to low. Continue cooking at a gentle simmer until the calamari is fully tender and is easily pierced with a fork, about 30 minutes. Taste and adjust the seasoning, then add the okra and lemon juice. Cook until the okra is fork-tender but still slightly crunchy to the bite, another 5 minutes. Serve hot over the rice or another grain of your choice, with sauce dah on the side (if using).

STEAMED COD LIBOKE

SERVES 2 ♊

Liboke, which originated in the Congo, is easy to prepare and fun to serve. It uses a method known as *en papillote,* in which the food (usually fish) is wrapped in a little parcel, allowing it to steam in its own juice. In West Africa, the fish is typically wrapped in banana leaves, but you can use aluminum foil or parchment paper and get the same effect.

LANGUAGE MATTERS

In principle, I love the mixing and blending of languages in everyday conversation. My daughter, Naia, for example, says "yeah" like an American teenager, "non" like a French toddler, and "kai fi"—come here!—to our dog, Malcolm, in perfect Wolof. And if you go to Senegal, you'll hear people all around you speaking both French and Wolof, seamlessly switching from the language that represents our heritage to the language that our colonizers used. Commonly used words and languages help us communicate to more people, *and* it's also so important to acknowledge and recognize the origin stories and histories of local terms and phrases. I find this to be ever more important as food cultures evolve and adapt, as many of the recipes in this book have done.

For example, the cod recipe on this page is called liboke in the Lingala language used in large parts of Central Africa, notably around the Congo, but is also referred to as *en papillote* (in paper), which is the commonly used French term for food steamed inside an enclosed parcel. Using African food names enhances and broadens visibility, which is key to trending toward a more equitable and balanced worldview. To set the trend in the right direction, in this book I try to always offer the African recipe name where there is one. My hope is that one day people will hear liboke instead of en papillote and immediately know what it is.

1 cup thinly sliced yellow onion

2 (6-ounce) cod fillets

4 plum tomatoes, chopped

2 teaspoons minced garlic

1 teaspoon grated fresh ginger

1 tablespoon chopped fresh thyme

1 teaspoon fine sea salt

½ teaspoon freshly ground black pepper

4 thin rounds of lemon

1 tablespoon olive or vegetable oil

Preheat the oven to 450°F.

Cut one 36-inch-long sheet of aluminum foil into 2 large rectangles (each 18 inches long). Fold each of the rectangles in half widthwise, then open it up. In the center of one side, layer half of the onion. Place one cod fillet on the onion, then top with half each of the tomatoes, garlic, and ginger. Season with half the thyme, ½ teaspoon salt, and ¼ teaspoon pepper, then top with 2 lemon rounds. Drizzle with half of the olive oil. Fold the other side over and crimp the edges tightly closed. Repeat with the remaining vegetables and fish on the other piece of foil. Place the fish packages on a sheet pan and bake until the fish is cooked through, about 10 minutes. Transfer each fish packet to a plate and serve immediately, allowing each diner to open the packet themselves.

HOT PÉPÉ SOUP

SERVES 4 ꞰꞰꞰꞰ

Hangovers. They happen even to the very best of us, and unfortunately, the only way out is through. Lucky for you, I have a remedy that I hope will help ease your pain. *Pépé* is West African pidgin English for "pepper." This soup is a formidable cure for those challenging days post–wild night out (trust me, I've been there, too!)—but you've got to be able to stand the heat. This is a spicy dish, and there's no way around that, unless you remove the habanero—it'll still be tasty, but you can't really call it a pépé soup anymore.

4 cups fish stock or water

½ cup finely chopped yellow onion

1 tablespoon grated fresh ginger

3 or 4 garlic cloves, as needed, minced

1 habanero or Scotch bonnet chili (sliced, if you like it extra spicy)

1 bay leaf

2 teaspoons ground dried crayfish or shrimp (see page 34) or 2 tablespoons fish sauce

1 teaspoon ground white pepper

1 pound tilapia or red snapper fillet, cut into large 2-inch chunks

½ pound medium shrimp, peeled and deveined

½ pound bay scallops

Fine sea salt

2 scallions, thinly sliced, for serving

2 tablespoons chopped fresh basil (preferably Thai basil), for serving

1 lemon, cut into wedges, for serving

In a large pot, combine the fish stock, onion, ginger, garlic, habanero, bay leaf, crayfish powder, and white pepper, and bring to a boil over high heat. Reduce the heat to low and simmer, stirring occasionally with a wooden spoon, for 5 minutes. Add the tilapia, shrimp, and scallops. Return to a boil over high heat. Reduce the heat to low and simmer until the seafood is cooked and fragrant, another 6 to 8 minutes. Add salt to taste and stir to incorporate. Use the back of the wooden spoon to crush the habanero into the broth to release the spiciness. (The more you crush, the spicier it will be.) Serve hot in bowls, topped with the scallions and basil, with lemon wedges on the side to squeeze into the soup.

AROMATICS

When cooking soups and stews in West Africa, some recipes begin with directly immersing the aromatics (onions, ginger, garlic, spices, or herbs) in a liquid (water or stock)—no sautéing or "sweating" the aromatics needed. This method of direct infusion is actually a great way to capture the flavors of the aromatics. As they cook, the essences of the aromatics are extracted, adding big flavors to the cooking liquid. It is also a healthy way to use less oil in your cooking.

CHARRED COD WITH GARLICKY PARSLEY ROF

SERVES 4 ʌʌʌʌ

On the busiest of my busy days, I'm running from eight hours of meetings to playing with Naia to walking Malcolm, the dog, to rushing to the kitchen to cook dinner for the family. It's days like these that I'm so grateful for recipes that don't require a lot of prep or cook time. This dish is simply delicious and deliciously simple. It's made by slathering garlicky parsley rof on broiled cod. The refreshing sensation of the rof, paired with the rustic charred whitefish, is just perfect. Serve this with some salad greens for a satisfying, no-fuss midweek meal.

4 (6-ounce) skin-on, boneless cod fillets

1 teaspoon fine sea salt

1 teaspoon freshly ground black pepper

2 tablespoons extra-virgin olive oil

¼ cup Garlicky Parsley Rof (page 49)

1 lemon, cut into wedges, for serving

Preheat the oven broiler to high.

Sprinkle the fillets with the salt and pepper and brush them all over with the oil. Place the fillets, skin-side up, on an oven-safe sheet pan and cook until the skin has a nice charred color and the flesh flakes easily with a fork (and registers 140° to 145°F), 2 to 3 minutes (depending on the thickness of the fillets). Remove from the oven and generously drizzle the rof over the fish. Serve immediately, with lemon wedges on the side.

VEGETABLES

**NOT JUST A
SIDE HUSTLE**

VEGETABLES

When I was a kid, my mom (who had five children to feed at every single meal) would teach us values like patience and contentment as we ate around a bowl. "Imagine there is a triangle in front of you," she would say. "This triangle is your own section to eat from." The meat, usually placed in the center of the bowl, was off-limits until mom distributed it equally into everyone's triangle after we finished our veggies and grains. Because we ate our vegetables first, when we were the hungriest, we grew to love the diversity of colors, flavors, and textures that the vegetables provided us daily. (Naia, my Senegalese-Japanese-Chinese daughter who is growing up in Northern California, has somehow inherited a viscerally African understanding of the role of vegetables in her diet. Whenever we serve her dinner in her little plastic divided plate, she reaches immediately for the greens—which she calls "leaf!"—and the tomatoes—"malo." And she loves okra and seaweed. Go figure!)

It's only in modern industrial times that people have gotten used to eating, say, a large steak occupying most of the plate with a small salad and/or fries on the side. To me, this still feels like a somewhat strange, not very efficient way of eating. Plant-based ingredients play a critical role in creating the West African palate, and they—not the meat—bear the responsibility for bringing out some of the most iconic flavors of our cuisine, along with providing vital nutrition and satisfaction. And so, in this very special, vegetables-at-front-and-center chapter, I introduce you to a range of yummy, healthy, hearty vegetarian dishes that will nourish your soul and check off all your vitamin and mineral boxes. I'll take you to Cameroon, from which I drew inspiration for the delectable Cameroon-Inspired Eggplant Stew (page 184); to Nigeria with the Pumpkin Seed "Egusi" Stew with Eggplant and Collard Greens (page 180) and Spinach and Mushroom Efo Riro (page 182); and Côte d'Ivoire with the Baked Ginger-Chili Plantain Kelewele (page 179). I go to Brazil and back with the Coconut Collard Greens with Butternut Squash (page 162). And, of course, I've included the Root Vegetable Mafé (page 188), which I discuss at the beginning of this book (see page 55) as the recipe that started me on my quest to bring West African food to the world.

COCONUT COLLARD GREENS WITH BUTTERNUT SQUASH

SERVES 4 AS A SIDE DISH ⅄⅄⅄⅄

I love cooking with coconut milk. It has the perfect consistency for making vegetable dishes filling and rich and can be either sweet or savory. It's also good for our immune, cardiac, and digestive systems. This recipe uses coconut milk as a base for cooking collard greens, a popular leafy green in West Africa, the American South, and many other parts of the African diaspora. Add in the butternut squash and you have an elegant, unforgettable dish that just might change the way you think about vegan food forever.

1 pound collard greens, stemmed and cut into 1-inch strips

2 tablespoons sustainably sourced red palm oil (see page 31) or vegetable oil

1 small yellow onion, chopped

2 garlic cloves, minced

1 tablespoon grated fresh ginger

1 small butternut squash, peeled and diced into ½-inch pieces (about 2 cups)

1½ cups or 1 (13.5-ounce) can unsweetened full-fat coconut milk

1 tablespoon fresh lemon juice

1 teaspoon fine sea salt, plus more as needed

1 teaspoon freshly ground black pepper, plus more as needed

½ teaspoon ground turmeric

½ teaspoon cayenne pepper

3 scallions, thinly sliced, for serving

¼ cup chopped fresh cilantro, for serving

Bring a large pot of water to a boil over high heat. Add the collard greens, reduce the heat to medium-low, and simmer, partially covered, until very soft and tender, about 1 hour. Drain well and set aside. (See Note on page 181.)

In a large pot, heat the oil over medium heat. Add the onion and cook until fragrant and soft, about 2 minutes. Add the garlic and ginger, and cook, stirring with a wooden spoon, until fragrant, another 2 minutes. Add the butternut squash, coconut milk, lemon juice, salt, pepper, turmeric, and cayenne. Stir and bring to a simmer. Reduce the heat to low and cook until the squash is easily pierced with a fork, about 15 minutes. Add the cooked collard greens and stir to combine. Taste and adjust the seasoning with salt and pepper as needed. Top with the scallions and cilantro and serve.

PORTOBELLO MUSHROOM DIBI

SERVES 4 ᴀᴀᴀᴀ

Just the thought of serving dibi makes me want to call up all my best friends and invite them over for dinner. The cooking method for this steamed dish resembles the wrap-and-steam method used at the dibiterie (see page 100) or for the Steamed Cod Liboke (page 153). The dibiteries use kraft paper, but here I use aluminum foil because it's something everyone has in their pantry. While the portobello mushrooms are roasting in the oven, their musky goodness makes friends with the spices and onion juices, then they greet your guests with a dramatic poof of aromatic steam when you unwrap the packets in front of them.

2 pounds portobello mushrooms (8 to 10 mushrooms), stemmed, cut into 1-inch-thick slices

½ cup coarsely chopped yellow onion

2 tablespoons chopped fresh thyme

2 tablespoons extra-virgin olive oil, plus more for brushing the foil

2 to 4 garlic cloves, as needed, thinly sliced or chopped

1 teaspoon fine sea salt

½ teaspoon freshly ground black pepper

Crusty baguette, for serving

Cut a sheet of aluminum foil into eight 12 × 12-inch squares and stack them in groups of 2, so you have 4 stacks of foil.

In a large bowl, combine the mushrooms, onion, thyme, oil, garlic, salt, and pepper. Mix well using your hands or a wooden spoon.

Preheat the oven to 400°F.

Brush one square of each foil stack with oil, then divide the mushrooms among the 4 oiled squares. Fold both squares in each stack over and crimp the edges together to seal into packets. Place the foil packets on a sheet pan and bake in the oven for 20 to 25 minutes. (After 20 minutes, remove one packet from the oven to check for doneness: The mushrooms and onion should be tender and juicy.) Place the contents of each packet on a plate or bowl for serving, or eat the mushrooms directly from the packets. Serve with the baguette.

CRISPY CASSAVA CAKES

SERVES 4 𐐒𐐒𐐒𐐒

Like many of the best fried foods in the world, these hearty and savory croquettes are crisp on the outside and moist on the inside. The cassava is boiled and mashed, which gives it a natural hold so you don't need to use any eggs to bind it—and means it's completely vegan. The scallions give it a great kick that instantly wakes up your taste buds. I recommend serving these patties with a heaping pile of greens for the perfect meal on days when you feel like eating light without compromising on joy and flavor.

1 pound peeled fresh or frozen cassava, cut into 2-inch chunks

2 scallions, chopped

1 tablespoon finely chopped cilantro

½ teaspoon fine sea salt

¼ teaspoon freshly ground black pepper

2 tablespoons melted coconut oil or extra-virgin olive oil, plus a little more for your hands

Everyday Hot Pepper Kani Sauce (page 59), for serving (optional)

1 lime, cut into wedges, for serving

In a large pot, add the cassava and enough water to cover the cassava by 2 inches. Bring the water to a boil over high heat and cook until very soft, 20 to 30 minutes. Drain and remove any hard, fibrous bits. Transfer back to the pot and add the scallions, cilantro, salt, and pepper. Mash until smooth and allow the mixture to cool. Put a little oil on the palms of your hands (this will prevent the cassava from sticking), then shape the cassava mixture into 4 patties about 1 inch thick.

In a large heavy-bottomed skillet, heat the 2 tablespoons oil over medium-high heat. Carefully transfer the cassava patties to the oil and cook until golden and crisp on both sides, 2 to 3 minutes per side. Transfer to serving plates.

Serve immediately with the kani sauce (if using) and lime wedges on the side.

CHARRED SWEET POTATOES

SERVES 4 AS A SIDE DISH ♀♀♀♀

This beautifully sweet and spicy side dish brings me right back to those little coastal restaurants in Dakar where you can sit for hours catching up with a friend while gazing out at the horizon. It's the perfect accompaniment to a great conversation over steak or roast chicken. It has the flavors, colors, and vibe of a dish that might have been grilled over an open flame, but without all the fuss. I achieve this effect by first boiling the unpeeled potatoes and then splitting them in half and broiling them. The garlicky parsley rof blends so well with the caramelized sweet potato—you might want to make extra, because it always has people reaching for seconds.

2 medium sweet potatoes (about ½ pound), rinsed
2 tablespoons extra-virgin olive oil, for drizzling
¼ cup Garlicky Parsley Rof (page 49), for serving

In a large pot, add the sweet potatoes and enough water to cover the sweet potatoes by 2 inches. Bring to a boil over high heat. Reduce the heat to medium-low and continue cooking until the sweet potatoes are easily pierced with a fork, about 30 minutes. Drain and set aside. When the sweet potatoes are cool enough to handle, use a knife to split each sweet potato lengthwise into 2 halves.

Preheat the oven broiler to high.

Place the sweet potatoes, cut-side up, in a broiler-proof dish. Drizzle a little oil on the cut part of each sweet potato half and place the sweet potatoes under the broiler until the tops begin to burn, 3 to 4 minutes. Spoon the rof over the tops and serve hot.

COMFORTING CAULIFLOWER, RED BEAN, AND DATE SALAD

SERVES 4 ♁♁♁♁

I'm a strong believer in food as a source of love and comfort. In many cultures, including mine and Lisa's, love is commonly expressed not through words or physical affection but through cooking—whether that's a grandmother preparing a meal for her entire family or a dad teaching a toddler some kitchen basics (as is the case in my home). For us, this hearty vegan meal is the perfect starter recipe for anyone who wants to flex their food-as-love-language muscle. The cauliflower, which can be boring and unappealing without the right treatment, is roasted to perfection until it's almost caramelized. It's then mixed with red beans and tossed with my signature ginger dressing. The dates give it a surprise sweetness that plays with the heat of the ginger. This one-bowl meal is the ideal blend of textures and flavors to bring some sweetness and spice into your home.

1 small head of cauliflower, cut into florets (about 2 pounds)

3 tablespoons extra-virgin olive oil, for drizzling

1 teaspoon fine sea salt, plus more as needed

½ teaspoon freshly ground black pepper, plus more as needed

2 cups chopped romaine lettuce (2-inch pieces)

1½ cups cooked red beans or 1 (15.5-ounce) can, rinsed and drained

1 cup coarsely chopped pitted dates

½ cup Ginger Vinaigrette (page 42)

¼ cup shelled pumpkin seeds, toasted

¼ cup thinly sliced red onion

Preheat the oven to 425°F. Line a large sheet pan with parchment paper.

Place the cauliflower florets on the parchment-lined sheet pan, drizzle with the oil, and toss together. Season with the salt and pepper. Roast until the florets are tender and browned around the edges, 25 minutes. Let the cauliflower cool.

In a large bowl, combine the roasted cauliflower, romaine, beans, dates, vinaigrette, pumpkin seeds, and red onion. Transfer to a serving platter or bowl. Taste and adjust the seasoning as needed.

GREEN BEANS WITH RED SAUCE

SERVES 4 AS A SIDE DISH ⅄⅄⅄⅄

This easy and flavorful recipe combines my version of the Ghanaian red sauce with fresh green beans. Red sauce, one of our mother sauces (see page 51), is used as a base for many great West African classics, and it's also a quick and welcome complement to your everyday serving of vegetables. In our household, we eat green beans often because they're healthy, incredibly easy to digest, and popular with both adults and kids. Here, I roast the green beans instead of boiling them, to bring out their natural sweetness and a slightly charred flavor.

1 pound green beans or haricots verts, trimmed

2 teaspoons extra-virgin olive oil

½ teaspoon fine sea salt

¼ teaspoon freshly ground black pepper

1 cup West African Red Sauce (page 51), warmed

Preheat the oven to 425°F. Line a large sheet pan with parchment paper and set aside.

Wash the green beans and pat them dry, then transfer them to a large bowl. Toss with the oil to coat and season with the salt and pepper. Place the beans in a single layer on the parchment-lined sheet pan. Roast the beans in the oven until they are crisp, tender, and slightly caramelized, 15 minutes. Transfer to a bowl, add the red sauce, and toss to combine, if desired. Serve hot.

COOKING FOR OUR PLANET

In many ways, walking through bustling farmers' markets in California reminds me of some of the best food-shopping experiences I've had in West Africa: like the Buea Central Market in Cameroon with its vibrant music, colorful wax cloth-clad women with heavy baskets balanced on their heads, and rows of bountiful food products like pineapples, giant, sweet cassava leaves, and moringa. And the narrow market alleys at Kinshasa's Marché Central, the largest market in the Congo, where you can stock up on all the groceries and delicacies that you might possibly need for the week ahead, from beef bones for making broth to honey straight from the beehive.

As a mixed race, multicultural, environmentally conscious family living in America, we are committed to diversity of all kinds—racial, cultural, ecological—in order to turn the trajectory of this planet and its people around for the better. And as a chef, I'm a staunch advocate of culinary diversity, especially in making sure we utilize nature's various fruits and vegetables through the food we eat and the plants we surround ourselves with. Without a diversified diet, we literally can't survive. Too much of anything, even the seemingly healthiest things, like vitamin C–packed fruits, can cause imbalances in our bodies. Our planet's survival also depends on biodiversity. Thousands of nutritious and resilient plant species have become extinct because we've razed their habitats and ignored their value to our environment and diets.

Lisa and I count our blessings every day for the environmental diversity that we get to experience in our community. On any given day, we come home from a walk around the block with pockets full of fresh plums, every kind of citrus imaginable, pineapple guava, blackberries, rosemary, thyme, and lavender. Outside our windows at night, owls serenade each other and turkeys graze along the open road. In many ways, my life in Northern California feels so much like the summers I spent in Casamance, where people and nature coexisted mindfully, lovingly.

Whether you live near a grassy park, grow your own home vegetable garden, or have some potted herbs on your windowsill, there are always ways that you can connect with nature in your everyday life and bring a broad array of nutritional flavors into your diet. Ask yourself: Where can I create magic in my lived environment? How can I deepen my connection to the natural world?

CRISPY ROASTED HARISSA BRUSSELS SPROUTS

SERVES 4 AS A SIDE DISH ⋏⋏⋏⋏

Food has the ability to transcend borders, and flavors from one corner of the map can make their way quite seamlessly into other regions. It's this blending of cultures and tastes that makes our world more interesting and inclusive. North and West Africa have been borrowing each other's cooking techniques for centuries, and harissa (a North African chili paste) is an ingredient that I find myself happily reaching for often. Brussels sprouts are a popular snack that we often see on the appetizer menu at restaurants in New York and California, and making this dish will only reaffirm why: The crispy, caramelized texture of the deeply roasted sprouts with the irresistibly sweet and spicy kick of harissa will no doubt have you (and anyone lucky enough to be sharing this with you) reaching for just one more, and then just one more, and maybe just one last piece . . . until they're all gone.

HARISSA GLAZE

1 tablespoon vegetable oil

1 garlic clove, minced

2 tablespoons honey

2 tablespoons harissa (see page 35)

Zest from 1 lemon plus 3 tablespoons juice

BRUSSELS SPROUTS

1 pound Brussels sprouts, trimmed and halved

2 tablespoons extra-virgin olive or coconut oil

½ teaspoon fine sea salt, plus more as needed

¼ teaspoon freshly ground black pepper

Preheat the oven to 400°F.

PREPARE THE HARISSA GLAZE: In a small sauté pan, heat the vegetable oil and garlic over medium-high heat. Cook until the garlic begins to brown slightly, 1 minute. Add the honey, harissa, and lemon zest and juice, and whisk to combine. Reduce the heat to low and simmer until slightly thickened, 2 to 3 minutes.

PREPARE THE BRUSSELS SPROUTS: In a large bowl, combine the Brussels sprouts, olive oil, salt, and pepper, and mix. Transfer to a large sheet pan and spread out in a single layer. Roast in the oven, shaking the pan halfway through cooking, until the Brussels sprouts are crisp and charred on the outside and tender on the inside, about 40 minutes.

Transfer the Brussels sprouts to a bowl and toss with 2 tablespoons of the harissa glaze. Taste and adjust the seasoning with salt as needed. Serve hot. Store the remaining harissa glaze in a resealable jar with a tight-fitting lid in the refrigerator for up to one week.

BAKED GINGER-CHILI PLANTAIN KELEWELE

SERVES 6 AS A SIDE DISH ⩕⩕⩕⩕⩕⩕

I first crafted this sweet-and-spicy must-try plantain recipe for a benefit event for the New York Common Pantry, a hardworking nonprofit committed to ending hunger in the city. It is now a reigning favorite of the crowds that frequent my restaurant, Teranga, where my incredible sous-chef, Hamidou Dabre, makes batches of this delicious dish to ensure that everybody who walks through the doors of my restaurant gets to fill their plates with it. This version of kelewele has the same ginger-cayenne seasoning as the traditional version, but it is baked instead of fried, making it easier to prepare and healthier to eat. Serve as a side dish with grilled steak or Maman's Crispy Herb-Crusted Chicken (page 131).

6 plantains, ripe but firm

3 tablespoons olive or vegetable oil

1 tablespoon grated fresh ginger

1 teaspoon cayenne pepper

1 teaspoon fine sea salt

Preheat the oven to 375°F.

Slice the ends off each plantain and then make a long slit, from tip to tip, along the skin of each plantain to allow the steam to escape during baking (or else they may burst). Place the plantains (skin still on) on a sheet pan and cover tightly with aluminum foil. Bake the plantains until soft, about 40 minutes.

Meanwhile, in a small bowl, combine the oil, ginger, cayenne, and salt. Mix well and set aside.

Remove the baking dish from the oven and uncover the dish; leave the oven on. Allow the plantains to cool until they are easy to handle. Peel off and discard the skin from the plantains on the sheet pan, then brush the flesh with the ginger-cayenne mixture. Return the sheet pan to the oven until the plantains are slightly brown, about 10 more minutes. Serve immediately, whole or sliced.

PUMPKIN SEED "EGUSI" STEW WITH EGGPLANT
AND COLLARD GREENS

SERVES 6 ⋀⋀⋀⋀⋀⋀

When I serve this dish to my more carnivorous friends, they're always pleasantly surprised that a vegan dish can be so . . . meaty. This stew is based on egusi, an all-time favorite dish that originates from the Yoruba people, forty-five million strong and with its biggest concentration in Nigeria. Traditionally, the dish is made with seeds from egusi, a type of melon that grows abundantly in West Africa (see page 35). The seeds are cooked in red palm oil with leafy greens and various cuts of meat, like goat, beef, and chicken. In this recipe, I swap the egusi seeds for the more readily available pumpkin seeds, and the eggplant and collard greens substitute for the meat.

The fermented flavors of dawadawa add a unique umami, which I absolutely love, but if you want a simpler stew, you can skip it, or use fish sauce, if you don't mind the dish not being vegan. Whatever you decide, I'm confident it will be delicious and delightful.

1 cup stemmed and coarsely chopped collard greens

1 red bell pepper, coarsely chopped

1 cup chopped yellow onion

2 garlic cloves

1 teaspoon grated fresh ginger

1 habanero or Scotch bonnet chili, seeded and roughly chopped

1 cup raw shelled pumpkin seeds

½ cup sustainably sourced red palm oil (see page 31) or vegetable oil

1 cup coarsely chopped eggplant (1-inch cubes)

2 tablespoons dawadawa powder (see page 34) or 2 teaspoons fish sauce (optional)

2 teaspoons smoked paprika

4 cups vegetable stock or water

1 teaspoon fine sea salt

Fufu (page 228) or cooked rice, for serving

In a medium pot, bring 4 cups of water to a boil over high heat. Add the collard greens, reduce the heat to medium-low, and simmer, partially covered, until very soft and tender, about 1 hour. Drain well and set aside. (See Note.)

Using a food processor or mortar and pestle, blend or mash together the bell pepper, ½ cup of the onion, the garlic, ginger, and habanero until the mixture becomes a thick paste. Transfer to a medium bowl, then set aside.

Rinse the food processor and add the pumpkin seeds with the remaining ½ cup onion. Mix well until it becomes a thick paste.

In a large saucepan, heat the oil over medium-high heat. Add the eggplant and sauté, stirring with a wooden spoon, until soft, about 10 minutes. Add the dawadawa (if using) and paprika and stir for 1 more minute. Add the habanero mixture, stir well, and cook until the mixture combines, about 5 minutes. Add the pumpkin seed mixture and stir to combine, about 1 minute. Add the vegetable stock and salt, and bring to a boil over high heat. Reduce the heat to low and simmer, with the pot lid slightly ajar, until the stew has thickened a bit, about 10 minutes. Taste and adjust the seasoning as needed, then stir in the cooked collard greens. Serve hot with fufu or the starch of your choice.

NOTE: A few recipes in this book call for long-cooked collard greens, and a great shortcut is to make a big batch, then store them in small batches for future use. After cooking the collard greens, drain and drop them in a large bowl of ice water to cool. Drain again, then squeeze them in a towel to remove excess moisture. Store the leaves in a small reusable bag in the refrigerator for up to 3 days or in the freezer for up to 12 months. When ready to use, simply drop the leaves (cold or frozen) into the pot with the rest of the stew and cook until hot. Additionally, ½ teaspoon of baking soda added to the boiling water will help the greens stay greener.

SPINACH AND MUSHROOM EFO RIRO

SERVES 4 AAAA

I highly recommend that you try this recipe the next time a friend from Nigeria comes over, because you'll get instant street cred. Or a friend from anywhere, for that matter, because the dish is healthy, hearty, and delicious. This Yoruban stew is a staple of almost all Nigerian households. I use spinach as a substitute for the more traditional amaranth leaves, which are less easy to find in many parts of the world. (But if you can find amaranth leaves, by all means feel free to use them.) To make my version vegan but still hearty, I use portobello mushrooms instead of more typically used goat meat or beef.

2 coarsely chopped plum tomatoes

1 red bell pepper, chopped

1 habanero or Scotch bonnet chili, seeded and chopped

1 large yellow onion, coarsely chopped

½ cup sustainably sourced red palm oil (see page 31)

2 cups thickly sliced portobello mushrooms, cleaned and stemmed

1 tablespoon tomato paste

1 teaspoon fine sea salt

½ teaspoon freshly ground black pepper

1 cup vegetable stock or water

8 cups coarsely chopped fresh or 8 ounces frozen spinach or amaranth leaves

Fufu (page 228) or cooked rice, for serving

In a blender or food processor, add the tomatoes, bell pepper, habanero, and half of the chopped onion, and blend on medium speed until the mixture has reached a chunky consistency.

In a large pot, heat the oil over medium heat. Add the mushrooms and sauté, stirring occasionally, until soft, about 5 minutes. Add the remaining onion and cook, stirring, until softened, about 2 minutes. Add the tomato paste, reduce the heat to low, and stir well with a wooden spoon until the mixture turns a dark

red color, 2 to 3 minutes. Raise the heat to medium-low, add the tomato mixture, and cook, while stirring, until incorporated, 1 minute. Add the salt and pepper, and cook until thickened, 5 more minutes.

Raise the heat to high, add the vegetable stock, and bring to a boil. Stir in the spinach, then reduce the heat to medium-low and simmer until the spinach has wilted and the stew is thickened, 2 to 3 minutes. Serve with fufu or the starch of your choice.

CAMEROON-INSPIRED EGGPLANT STEW

SERVES 4 ⋀⋀⋀⋀

This recipe came about during a conversation I had with Christian Abegan, a chef from Cameroon, a beautiful country bordering both Central and West Africa that is known for its incredible diversity—of its ecosystem, its people, and, of course, its food. Christian and I talked for what felt like hours about the vast variety of eggplants that exist in Africa: tiny eggplants the size of kumquats, bitter eggplants shaped like beefsteak tomatoes, small round eggplants similar to Thai eggplants, classic globe-shaped eggplants found in every grocery store. Each can be prepared and presented in many different ways. His description of this classic Cameroonian eggplant dish stuck with me for its understated elegance. It's often made with smoked fish and dried shrimp, but this vegan version is just as good. If you can find Thai eggplants, those are closer in texture to the type of African eggplant used in the traditional recipe. In Africa, we also use scent leaf, a popular aromatic native herb also known as African basil, but you can use Thai basil, or if that's hard to find, Italian basil will do just fine.

2 large eggplants or 10 Thai eggplants, peeled and cut in 2-inch cubes (about 8 cups)

6 plum tomatoes, coarsely chopped, or 1 (14.5-ounce) can whole peeled tomatoes, drained

4 shallots, finely chopped

2 garlic cloves, finely chopped

1 teaspoon fine sea salt

½ teaspoon freshly ground black pepper

2 tablespoons chopped fresh Thai or Italian basil, for serving

In a large pot, place the eggplants and 2 cups of water. Bring to a boil over high heat, then reduce the heat to low. Simmer, stirring occasionally with a wooden spoon, until the water is completely absorbed, about 15 minutes. Stir in the tomatoes, shallots, garlic, salt, and pepper. Add 2 more cups of water, bring to a boil over high heat, then reduce the heat to medium. Simmer, gradually crushing the eggplants and tomatoes with a wooden spoon, until reduced to a thick mixture, another 30 minutes. Stir in the basil and serve immediately.

ROOT VEGETABLE MAFÉ PAGE 188

ROOT VEGETABLE MAFÉ

SERVES 4 TO 6 ⋒⋒⋒⋒

The scent of mafé instantly takes me back to my childhood. The peanut-based sauce, also one of the mother sauces of West African cuisine (see page 50), has some similarities with Mexican mole in that it is a nut-based sauce thickened through slow cooking. The classic West African mafé almost always has lamb, chicken, or fish, but I love the simplicity and elegance of the vegan version that I'm introducing here. My mafé overflows with healthy, delicious root vegetables like cassava, carrots, sweet potatoes, and turnips. It's the perfect one-pot choice when you're entertaining a mix of guests that includes really hungry people with various dietary restrictions.

Traditionally, the vegetables are cooked together in the same pot with the sauce, but I prefer to blanch the various vegetables (see facing page) because this allows me to have better control of the cooking of each individual vegetable. When they are ready to serve, I simply add them to the stew to finish cooking and to reheat. This also visibly enhances the natural colors and textures of the vegetables, making the dish that much more beautiful and presentable.

1 tablespoon peanut or vegetable oil

1 cup finely chopped yellow onion

2 teaspoons finely chopped garlic

1 heaping tablespoon tomato paste

2 cups unsweetened creamy peanut butter

4 cups vegetable stock or water

1 bay leaf

1 Scotch bonnet or habanero chili, left whole (optional)

1½ teaspoons fine sea salt

1 teaspoon freshly ground black pepper

1½ cups kosher salt, for blanching vegetables

4 medium carrots, cut into 2-inch chunks

½ pound peeled and cored fresh or frozen cassava or 1 large peeled russet potato, cut into 2- to 3-inch-thick wedges

2 medium turnips, peeled and cut into 1-inch-thick wedges (about ½ pound)

1 large sweet potato, peeled and cut into 1-inch cubes (about ½ pound)

10 medium okra pods, cut into ½-inch slices (optional)

Simply Fonio (page 215) or cooked rice, for serving

In a large pot, heat the oil over medium-high heat. Add the onion and garlic, and sauté until soft but not browned, about 5 minutes. Add the tomato paste and reduce the heat to low. Cook, stirring frequently with a wooden spoon, adding a few tablespoons of water as needed to keep the onion and garlic from scorching, until the tomato paste slightly darkens, about 5 minutes.

Add the peanut butter and stir well, using a wooden spoon, to combine. Add the vegetable stock, bay leaf, and Scotch bonnet (if using). Bring to a boil over high heat. Reduce the heat to low and simmer, stirring occasionally to fully dissolve the peanut butter. Season with the sea salt and pepper. Cook, stirring occasionally, until the oil rises to the surface, 15 to 20 minutes.

Meanwhile, in a large pot combine the kosher salt and 1 gallon of water and bring to a boil over high heat. Set a large bowl of ice water alongside. Drop the carrots, cassava, turnips, and sweet potato into the boiling water and blanch until they are just tender but still al dente, about 5 minutes (you may need to work in batches if your pot is not large enough). Using a large slotted spoon, transfer the vegetables to the ice water to stop the cooking, then drain and set them aside.

Add the blanched vegetables and okra (if using) to the peanut sauce and continue cooking until they are soft and easily pierced with a fork, about 10 minutes. Serve with a starch of your choice.

BLANCHING BRINGS OUT THE BEST

Stewing vegetables is relatively easy, but the one thing that you have to be careful of is overcooking. If you let the vegetables sit for too long in the stew as they cook, they can fall apart and lose their freshness, which will affect the way they look and taste when you serve them. Overcooking can also deprive these beautiful products of nature of their water-soluble nutrient content, like vitamins B, C, and folate. My technique for making sure that my veggies stay crisp and colorful is to blanch them separately as I prepare the base sauce. This is a great strategy, because you can cook everything to perfection without having to overthink timing and coordination.

OKRA WITH TOMATOES

SERVES 4 AS A SIDE DISH ⋏⋏⋏⋏

You can't go far in West Africa without encountering okra. It grows everywhere and is a vegetable staple of the region. It's also used as a thickening agent for soups and stews like Seafood Okra Soupou Kanja (page 137), Poached Calamari Caldou in Tomato and Lemon Broth (page 150), and Senegalese Ndambe Peasant Stew (page 210). I love the gooey-crunchy combination of textures that it naturally provides. This uncomplicated dish brings an African vegetable together with the trusty tomato in an elegant side dish that goes perfectly with rice, fonio (see page 215), or pretty much any fish recipe in this book.

2 tablespoons olive or vegetable oil

½ cup chopped yellow onion

2 cups diced plum tomatoes

2 garlic cloves, chopped

2 cups sliced fresh or frozen okra (1-inch slices)

½ teaspoon fine sea salt, plus more as needed

¼ teaspoon freshly ground black pepper, plus more as needed

¼ teaspoon cayenne pepper, plus more as needed

In a large skillet, heat the oil over medium-low heat. Add the onion and sauté until tender, about 3 minutes. Add the tomatoes and garlic, and cook until the tomatoes are soft, about 10 minutes. Add the okra and stir with a wooden spoon to combine. Allow the mixture to simmer until the okra is tender but still crunchy, another 5 minutes. Season with the salt, pepper, and cayenne, adding more to taste if desired. Serve immediately.

OKRA, A WEST AFRICAN COOK'S BEST FRIEND

I've heard every excuse about why people don't like okra, many of them along the lines of "It's too gooey" or "It's so slimy." Okra is not for everyone. I'll give you that. If you're anything like my little brother, Kiki, you might even hate it passionately. Kiki aside, though, a person's opinion of okra is one of the key indicators of how to spot a true African foodie. Everywhere across the African continent, from Cairo to Cape Town, you'll find at least one dish with okra as an ingredient. If you ask me, okra is the king of all African vegetables. Versatile and often used as a thickener for sauces and stews, it is a very special friend to West African cooks like me. Okra can be grilled, sautéed, braised, stewed, fried, roasted, or pickled. It's the main affair in one of my all-time favorite recipes, Seafood Okra Soupou Kanja (page 137), the original recipe behind the now-globally renowned Southern stew called gumbo. (Fun fact: The name gumbo is derived from the word *gombo,* which means "okra" in the Bantu language of West and Central Africa.)

For those who don't like the viscosity, you can cook the okra whole so the gooey middle doesn't get activated, or you can marinate it in vinegar and salt before cooking. Okra is best when it's young and tender without too many woodsy fibers to chew through. However you decide to take your okra, it is a nutrition powerhouse that's high in fiber and antioxidants, and an important symbol of health for the African diaspora. I personally cannot imagine my life without okra, and I am excited to share with you two of my favorite okra recipes in this chapter, Root Vegetable Mafé (page 188) and Okra with Tomatoes (opposite).

RED RED RED LOADED POTATOES

SERVES 2 AS A SIDE DISH 𝐀𝐀

Let's be honest. Who doesn't love to have a perfectly baked potato alongside their favorite meat dish? Here's a recipe that gives this classic accompaniment a quintessentially West African twist. The base of this recipe will feel familiar to those who have made baked potatoes before, but here they are topped with red red red, a beautiful stew filled with red beans and tomatoes that is just as good on its own but works so well as a potato filler that you might be skipping the sour cream, chives, and bacon bits for good.

2 large potatoes (any sweet potato variety or russet)

1 tablespoon olive or vegetable oil

1 cup Red Red Red (page 217), warmed

2 tablespoons coarsely chopped fresh cilantro, for serving (optional)

Preheat the oven to 425°F.

Using a fork, poke a few holes into the skin of the potatoes. Use a brush or your hands to coat the potatoes with the oil, and then put the potatoes straight onto the oven rack to roast until tender and easily pierced with a knife, 1 hour.

Split the potatoes in half lengthwise and then, with a fork, mash the flesh inside the skin. Spoon the red red red evenly over the top of both potatoes. Garnish with the cilantro (if using) and serve.

SAUTÉED CORN, SHIITAKE MUSHROOMS, AND CHERRY TOMATOES

Going to a barbecue and not sure what to take? This recipe is the solution for you. It's the ideal accompaniment to pretty much anything. The crunch of summer sweet corn paired with the tart, juicy burst of cherry tomatoes strikes the perfect, harmonious balance with the meaty, earthy shiitake. But it's the garlicky parsley rof that really makes the dish special and uniquely West African. This dish is incredibly easy to prepare, and I promise that yours will be the most popular dish at the party.

4 large cobs of sweet corn

2 tablespoons extra-virgin olive oil

1 cup thinly sliced shiitake mushrooms, cleaned and stemmed

1 cup quartered cherry tomatoes

3 tablespoons vegetable stock or water

½ teaspoon fine sea salt

¼ teaspoon freshly ground black pepper

2 tablespoons Garlicky Parsley Rof (page 49)

Remove the husks and silks from the corn and cut the kernels off the cobs (you should have about 2 cups). Place the corn in a medium bowl.

In a large skillet, heat the oil over medium-high heat. Add the mushrooms and sauté, stirring frequently with a wooden spoon, until tender and starting to brown, about 5 minutes. Add the corn kernels, tomatoes, vegetable stock, salt, and pepper, and continue cooking until the tomatoes soften and the liquid reduces, about 5 more minutes. Add the rof and stir to combine. Serve hot.

BLACK BEAN–CASSAVA VEGGIE BURGERS

MAKES 4 BURGERS

I make burgers for dinner fairly often at home. Because Naia is not a big meat eater, I decided to experiment with a new type of vegan burger that uses cassava as a binding agent. The shiitake mushrooms and cassava together give this recipe a nice, meaty texture, and the addition of black beans ups the protein quotient to make sure you feel satisfyingly full at the end of the meal. To add some uniqueness and flavor, I've included two possible topping options here: yassa for those days that call for a more savory burger situation, and Casamance salsa for when you want a fresh and tropical touch. It's also perfectly okay to simply dress your burger with any favorite additions like lettuce, tomato, ketchup, mustard, and mayo, too.

- ½ pound peeled fresh or frozen cassava
- 1 tablespoon olive or vegetable oil
- 1 cup finely chopped shiitake mushrooms, cleaned and stemmed
- ½ cup finely chopped yellow onion
- 3 garlic cloves, finely chopped
- 1 cup cooked black beans
- 1½ teaspoons cumin seeds, toasted
- 1 teaspoon fine sea salt
- ½ teaspoon freshly ground black pepper
- ¼ teaspoon cayenne pepper
- ¼ teaspoon smoked paprika
- 4 hamburger buns
- ¼ cup Classic Lemony Yassa Sauce (page 52) or Casamance Green Mango Salsa (page 53), for topping (optional)

In a large saucepan, add the cassava and enough water to cover by 2 inches. Bring to a boil over medium-high heat and cook until the cassava is very soft when poked with a fork, 25 to 30 minutes. Strain, transfer to a large bowl, and set aside to cool for 15 to 20 minutes. Remove and discard the hard center core of the cassava.

Preheat the oven to 375°F. Line a sheet pan with parchment paper and set aside.

In a large skillet, heat the oil over medium heat. Add the mushrooms, onion, and garlic, and sauté until the mushrooms and onion are soft, about 5 minutes.

Transfer to a large bowl or a food processor. Add the black beans, cassava, cumin seeds, salt, black pepper, cayenne, and paprika, then mash with a fork or pulse, leaving some of the beans intact. Divide the mixture into 4 portions, about ½ cup each, and form into patties using your hands. Place the patties on the parchment-lined sheet pan and bake until the outsides are crispy but not burned, flipping them once, 20 minutes total.

Place a burger on the bottom half of each bun, then top each patty with 1 tablespoon of the yassa sauce or salsa (if using), and the other half of the bun. Serve immediately.

FONIO, KALE, AND MANGO SALAD

SERVES 4 ⋏⋏⋏⋏

This colorful, easy-to-make salad is one of my favorites to demonstrate when I teach cooking classes, because it is both hard to mess up and a guaranteed crowd-pleaser. It's also a menu item that many who dine at my New York restaurant, Teranga, love to order and later rave about. The balance of the West African super grain fonio (see page 31), the dark, leafy kale greens, and the sometimes sweet, sometimes tart, always beautiful color and flavor of the mango is a joy to serve and delightful to taste.

2 cups chopped lacinato kale leaves (ribs removed, 1-inch pieces)

2 tablespoons extra-virgin olive oil

2 cups Simply Fonio (page 215)

1 cup quartered cherry tomatoes

½ cup diced mango

¼ cup thinly sliced red onion

¼ cup Ginger Vinaigrette (page 42)

½ teaspoon fine sea salt

¼ teaspoon freshly ground black pepper

In a large bowl, add the kale and gently rub it with the oil. Add the cooked fonio, the tomatoes, mango, and red onion. Toss with the vinaigrette, salt, and pepper, and serve.

ROASTED EGGPLANT
IN MAFÉ PEANUT SAUCE

SERVES 4 AS A SIDE DISH ᴀᴀᴀᴀ

This dish is a conversation between two of my favorite ingredients: eggplants and peanuts. It's my version of a dish that's been stuck in my memory ever since my friend Chef Mashama Bailey prepared it at Chef Kwame Onwuachi's Family Reunion. Eggplant, when roasted to perfection, offers a soft and juicy interior that complements its charred exterior. The combination of the creamy mafé peanut sauce and the crunchy crushed peanuts makes this the ultimate comfort side dish, one that gives new meaning to the phrase "Simple is best."

2 large eggplants (1½ to 2 pounds each)

¼ cup extra-virgin olive oil

1 teaspoon fine sea salt

½ teaspoon freshly ground black pepper

2 cups Mafé Peanut Sauce (page 50), warmed

½ cup crushed roasted peanuts, for serving

2 tablespoons fresh cilantro leaves, for serving

Preheat the oven to 450°F.

Cut off the stem ends of the eggplants, then, using a vegetable peeler or sharp knife, peel vertical strips off of the eggplant skins (like zebra stripes). Cut the peeled eggplants into 1-inch-thick rounds. Place the eggplant rounds on a large sheet pan (overlapping if necessary), brush the rounds with half the oil, and sprinkle half the salt and pepper evenly on top. Flip the rounds and repeat on the other side with the remaining oil, salt, and pepper.

Place the sheet pan in the oven and roast (without flipping) until the eggplant rounds are cooked through and soft but still hold their shape, and the edges are caramelized, about 30 minutes. Transfer the eggplant to a large plate or serving platter and allow it to cool for a few minutes. Generously spoon the warm mafé on each piece, sprinkle with the crushed peanuts and cilantro, and serve.

MASHED SWEET PLANTAINS

SERVES 4 AS A SIDE DISH ♙♙♙♙

Plantains, which grow abundantly in Southeast Asia, West and Central Africa, and parts of India and South America, are amazingly versatile. They can be sweet. They can be savory. They can be panfried, deep-fried, or baked. They can be eaten when they're still firm or when they're overripe. (I believe plantains are most delicious when their skin has started to blacken, unlike the common banana.) This recipe calls for the wonder fruit to be puréed. It uses only four ingredients and is a great complement to any meal, especially roasted chicken or fish. The chili-less version is also a perfect starter baby food, as my daughter, Naia, can attest.

3 ripe sweet plantains with dark spots on the skin, peeled and cut into 2-inch chunks

½ cup sustainably sourced red palm oil (see page 31) or extra-virgin olive oil

1 habanero or Scotch bonnet chili, seeded and chopped, or ½ teaspoon cayenne pepper (optional)

1 teaspoon fine sea salt

In a medium pot, place the plantains and add enough water to cover by 2 inches. Bring to a boil over high heat, then reduce the heat to medium and simmer until the plantains are tender when pierced with a fork, about 10 minutes. Drain well.

Return the plantains to the pot over low heat and cook, allowing any remaining water to evaporate, for about 1 minute. Gradually add the oil, 1 tablespoon at a time, while mashing the plantains with a wooden spoon. Add the habanero (if using) and stir. Remove from the heat and stir in the salt. Serve immediately while warm, on its own or as a side.

SONGHAI WATERCRESS AND WATERMELON SALAD

SERVES 4 AS A SIDE DISH ♈♈♈♈

This sweet and spicy salad is the perfect complement to a hot summer day. It's also a nod to the Songhai Empire of the fifteenth and sixteenth centuries, which in African history remains known as one of the largest states to have ever ruled the western Sahel. (Its main area of influence overlaps with what we now think of as the Sudan.) This recipe, a West African twist on a summer salad, centers around the watermelon, a fruit that arrived in the Americas from the same corner of the world that the Songhai came from. I imagine that once way back in the day, Songhai home cooks might have used watermelon in this way to create a refreshing appetizer for their families. It's a summertime favorite at my restaurant, Teranga, in New York City.

2 teaspoons honey

¼ cup whole raw cashews

1 tablespoon coarsely ground black pepper

¼ teaspoon crushed red pepper flakes

6 cups watercress (1 to 2 bunches, thick stems removed) or chopped romaine lettuce

1 cup diced seedless watermelon

1 cup quartered cherry tomatoes

½ cup seeded, 1-inch diced cucumber

¼ cup thinly sliced red onion

¼ cup Ginger Vinaigrette (page 42)

In a small skillet, add the honey and warm it over medium heat. Add the cashews, black pepper, and red pepper flakes and continue cooking until the honey and pepper coat the cashews and the liquid has almost evaporated, about 10 minutes. (Stir occasionally and reduce the heat as needed to prevent the honey from burning.) Remove from the heat and set aside to cool to room temperature.

In a large bowl, combine the watercress, watermelon, tomatoes, cucumber, and red onion. Add the vinaigrette and toss. When they are cool enough to handle, coarsely crush the cashews with the side of a chef's knife, and sprinkle over the top before serving.

VEGETABLE YASSA

SERVES 4 ᚠᚠᚠᚠ

This yassa sauce continues to be one of my most requested recipes, even after decades of my cooking professionally. Traditionally, yassa is served with fish or meat. Here, finally, is a vegan version that uses butternut squash, carrots, red bell peppers, and zucchini for a colorful, hearty meal for anyone to enjoy. Like any good yassa, it's lemony and briny in all the right ways, but without any of the meatiness.

1 medium butternut squash (about 2 pounds)

2 large carrots, cut into ½-inch-thick rounds

4 garlic cloves, finely chopped

3 tablespoons olive or vegetable oil

1 teaspoon fine sea salt

½ teaspoon freshly ground black pepper

1 large or 2 medium zucchini, cut into 1-inch-thick rounds

2 red bell peppers, cut into 1-inch pieces

2 cups Classic Lemony Yassa Sauce (page 52), warmed

Cooked rice or Simply Fonio (page 215), for serving

Preheat the oven to 400°F.

Using a sharp knife, cut off about ¼ inch from both ends of the butternut squash. With a sharp vegetable peeler, peel off the outer skin of the squash. Stand the squash upright and, again with a sharp knife, cut the squash in half from top to bottom. Using a spoon, scrape out the seeds and the fibrous pulp in the cavity. Cut the squash into 1-inch-thick cubes (you should have about 3 cups).

In a large bowl, combine the butternut squash, carrots, and half of the garlic. Drizzle with 2 tablespoons of the oil and season with ½ teaspoon of the salt and ¼ teaspoon of the pepper. Mix well to combine. Place the seasoned vegetables in a large cast-iron skillet (or

a sheet pan lined with aluminum foil) and roast in the oven until the vegetables begin to slightly caramelize on the edges, about 10 minutes.

While the butternut squash and carrots are cooking, combine the zucchini and bell peppers with the remaining garlic, 1 tablespoon oil, ½ teaspoon salt, and ¼ teaspoon pepper. Stir well to combine. Remove the skillet from the oven and place the zucchini and bell peppers over the top of the butternut squash and carrots. Return to the oven and roast until the squash and carrots are tender and easily pierced with a fork, 10 to 15 more minutes. Remove the vegetables from the oven and toss them in the yassa sauce. Serve with fonio or cooked rice.

BAKED PIRI-PIRI CAULIFLOWER

SERVES 4 ♈♈♈♈

Cauliflower is rich in fiber and full of antioxidants, and the little cloudlike bunches that it forms naturally are quite beautiful (especially those you get from the farmers' market). One of the best things to do with cauliflower is to bake it, and then broil it briefly, so you get this lovely, caramelized finish. And then, when you dress it up with piri-piri sauce, all of a sudden it takes on a life of its own, full of spice and sass, the great-tasting sidekick to a plate of fonio (see page 215).

1 large head of cauliflower, stem removed (about 2 pounds)

1 cup West African Piri-Piri Sauce (page 58)

3 tablespoons extra-virgin olive oil

½ teaspoon fine sea salt

1 tablespoon fresh cilantro leaves, for serving (optional)

Preheat the oven to 400°F.

In a cast-iron skillet or baking dish, place the head of cauliflower.

In a small bowl, combine the piri-piri sauce and oil. Pour all but 2 tablespoons of the piri-piri mixture over the cauliflower, making sure to cover the whole surface. Season with the salt, then place in the oven and bake until a knife easily pierces the core, 35 to 50 minutes.

Raise the oven temperature to its highest setting and roast until the top of the cauliflower turns a light brown color, 2 more minutes. Remove the skillet from the oven and let it cool for 5 minutes before serving. Top with the remaining piri-piri mixture, sprinkle with the cilantro (if using), and serve.

KABOCHA IN SWEET PEPPER "EGUSI" SAUCE

SERVES 4 ♀♀♀♀

The squash family is broad and vast, its members varying in size, shape, flavor, and texture. A favorite in our multicultural home is the kabocha, a type of winter squash also known as a Japanese pumpkin. Of all the many pumpkins and squashes in the world, kabocha is beloved for being exceptionally sweet and satisfyingly firm and meaty. This simple recipe takes all the magic of kabocha and brings it into perfect harmony with the sweet pepper egusi sauce for a quintessentially West African vegetarian delight.

1 medium kabocha squash (about 2 pounds), seeded and cut into 1-inch wedges (see Note)

2 tablespoons extra-virgin olive oil

2 teaspoons fine sea salt

1 teaspoon freshly ground black pepper

2 cups Sweet Pepper "Egusi" Sauce (page 60)

2 tablespoons shelled pumpkin seeds, toasted

2 tablespoons fresh cilantro leaves

Preheat the oven to 400°F. Line a large sheet pan with aluminum foil.

In a large bowl, toss the kabocha wedges with the oil and sprinkle with the salt and pepper. Place the wedges in a single layer on the foil-lined sheet pan and roast in the oven until the wedges are soft and caramelized on the edges, 30 minutes. Transfer to a serving platter, then drizzle the egusi sauce over the hot wedges. Sprinkle with the pumpkin seeds and cilantro and serve hot.

NOTE: The kabocha skin is very tough, but you shouldn't let that stop you from cooking with the kabocha. There are many ways to cut through the edible rind. An easy method is to soften the squash in the microwave for about 5 minutes or in a preheated 400°F oven for about 20 minutes. Then, cut the kabocha in half, remove the seeds, and cut it into wedges.

SENEGALESE NDAMBE PEASANT STEW

SERVES 4 ⋀⋀⋀⋀

In Senegal, ndambe is traditionally made with sweet potatoes and black-eyed peas, but here I use butternut squash instead of sweet potatoes to keep the sweetness to a minimum, and add okra as an option to make an extra-savory, more texturally complex and nutritious version that my family loves to eat at home. Ndambe stew can be served as a side dish for roasted chicken, with rice, or sandwiched between pieces of bread. On the streets of Dakar, breakfast joints known as tangana often serve ndambe in a baguette as a quick snack. When I traveled to Senegal with Anthony Bourdain to film an episode of *Parts Unknown,* this was his favorite thing to eat.

3 tablespoons vegetable oil

1 cup chopped yellow onion

1 cup diced plum tomatoes

1 tablespoon tomato paste

2 or 3 garlic cloves, as needed, minced

1 teaspoon minced fresh ginger

1 bay leaf

4 cups vegetable stock or water

2 cups peeled and diced fresh or frozen butternut squash (1-inch cubes)

1 habanero or Scotch bonnet chili, seeded and finely chopped

2 teaspoons fine sea salt

½ teaspoon freshly ground black pepper

2 cups cooked black-eyed peas or 1 (15.5-ounce) can, rinsed and drained

1 cup 1-inch slices fresh or frozen okra (optional)

In a large stainless-steel pot or Dutch oven, heat the oil over medium-high heat. Add the onion and cook until soft but not brown, about 3 minutes. Add the tomatoes, tomato paste, garlic, ginger, and bay leaf, and stir using a wooden spoon. Reduce the heat to medium-low and cook, stirring often to avoid scorching, until the mixture looks like a paste and the oil separates, 5 more minutes.

Add the vegetable stock, stir, and bring to a boil over high heat. Reduce the heat to medium-low and simmer until incorporated, about 10 minutes. Add the butternut squash, habanero, salt, and pepper. Continue cooking until the squash is easily pierced with a fork, about 10 minutes. Add the black-eyed peas and okra (if using), raise the heat to high to return to a boil, then reduce the heat to low and simmer until most of the liquid has been absorbed, 7 to 10 minutes. Serve immediately, while hot.

GRAINS

NO WEST AFRICAN MEAL IS COMPLETE WITHOUT THEM

NO WEST AFRICAN MEAL IS COMPLETE WITHOUT THEM

& BEANS

Where I come from, everyone knows that a generous helping of grains is an essential element of your plate. The African continent has more native grains than any other continent in the world. There are the usual suspects, like rice and barley, but also millet, sorghum, fonio, teff, and many more. Grains are the blank canvas onto which we create our eclectic landscape of meals. They are the foundations for many culinary masterpieces, bringing a sense of balance, soothing the intensity of the spices, absorbing the sop of the sauces.

Beans are a critical part of the food culture of the African diaspora no matter where we are in the world. Black-eyed peas are auspiciously served on New Year's Day in many Black households in America. People eat rice and beans in Ecuador, rice and peas in Jamaica, coconut and black-eyed pea waakye in Ghana. You also have bean stews, bean fritters, beans and plantains, bean porridge, bean everything. Whatever you call it, however you dress it up, there is no denying that grains and beans are at the root of our cuisine.

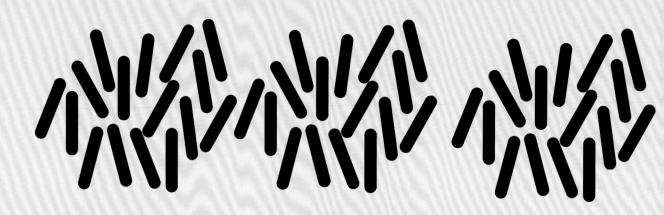

SIMPLY FONIO

SERVES 4

I am a big advocate of fonio. (You can read more about the benefits of this super grain on page 31. And my previous cookbook, *The Fonio Cookbook,* is dedicated entirely to recipes using this ingredient.) This recipe will ensure that you know how to make the perfect batch of fonio at home, for any occasion. Fonio is quite versatile, can complement pretty much any dish in this book, and literally takes about five minutes to cook. It's easier than cooking pasta or rice, and so much healthier, too. Make sure you buy cleaned, sustainably sourced fonio (a must for my company, Yolélé).

1 teaspoon fine sea salt

1 cup fonio

1 tablespoon extra-virgin olive oil (optional)

In a medium pot, bring 2 cups of water and the salt to a boil over high heat. Add the fonio and stir once. Reduce the heat to low and cover tightly. Cook until the water is absorbed and has evaporated, 3 to 5 minutes. Turn off the heat and keep the pot covered for another minute. Fluff with a fork and add the oil (if using). Serve warm.

RED RED RED
(RED BEAN–TOMATO STEW)

SERVES 6 ☺☺☺☺☺☺

This is my go-to, curl-up-on-the-couch-and-read-a-book comfort dish. The traditional version, called red red, is made with black-eyed peas, tomatoes, and red palm oil. I call my rendition red red red because I use red beans instead of black-eyed peas, which give this a richness of flavor and texture that you're sure to fall in love with. This is a great option for vegans as well as for omnivores who want a hearty, healthy meal that is relatively hands-off in its preparation. It's also great as a side dish with cooked rice or plantains.

2 cups dried red beans or 3 (15.5-ounce) cans, rinsed and drained

½ cup sustainably sourced red palm oil (see page 31) or vegetable oil

2 cups chopped yellow onion

1 red bell pepper, chopped

2 garlic cloves, finely chopped

1 tablespoon grated fresh ginger

2 tablespoons tomato paste

1 (28-ounce) can tomato purée or crushed tomatoes

1 habanero or Scotch bonnet chili, left whole (optional)

1 tablespoon curry powder

1 teaspoon smoked paprika

½ teaspoon fine sea salt, plus more as needed

½ pound smoked mackerel, skin off, bones removed, and cut into small pieces (optional)

In a large saucepan, add 8 to 10 cups of water and the red beans. Bring to a boil over high heat, then reduce the heat to low and simmer until the beans are soft, about 45 minutes. Drain and set aside. (If using canned beans, skip this step.)

While the beans are cooking, in a separate large pot, heat the oil over medium-high heat. Add the onions and sauté until softened, 5 to 8 minutes. Add the bell pepper, garlic, and ginger, and cook until softened, about 5 minutes. Stir in the tomato paste. Reduce the heat to low and cook, stirring occasionally to prevent the vegetables from scorching, until the paste starts to turn dark red, 2 to 3 minutes. Add the tomatoes, habanero (if using), curry powder, paprika, and salt, and stir well. Add the beans and the smoked mackerel (if using) to the pot and stir gently. Raise the heat to high and return to a boil, then reduce the heat to low and simmer until most of the liquid is absorbed, 10 more minutes. Remove the habanero and set it aside. Taste and adjust the seasoning before serving.

TRIPLE COCONUT WAAKYE RICE AND BEANS

SERVES 4 TO 6 AS A SIDE DISH

Rice and bean dishes are a mainstay throughout the African diaspora, and certainly in West Africa. Waakye hails from the Hausa people of Ghana and can be eaten for breakfast, lunch, or dinner. In the traditional recipe, the rice is cooked in water—sometimes with millet or sorghum stalks to infuse the dish with some darker color. I use coconut milk in this version, to add a luxurious and delicate flavor that you'll no doubt want to experience again and again and again. You can also add a bit of baking soda to darken the rice to get that same visual effect as from the millet straws, so I've included baking soda here as an option for you, too. For more texture, I garnish my waakye with dried coconut that I toast in a dry pan until fragrant and lightly browned. This versatile side pairs well with meat, fish, or vegetables. You can also eat it with a simple store-bought or homemade West African Red Sauce (page 51) served on top.

1 cup dried black-eyed peas or 2 (15.5-ounce) cans, rinsed and drained

2 cups jasmine rice, rinsed and drained

1 cup unsweetened full-fat coconut milk

½ cup chopped yellow onion

2 tablespoons dried coconut, plus 1 tablespoon, toasted, for serving

1 tablespoon melted coconut oil or extra-virgin olive oil

1 teaspoon fine sea salt, plus more as needed

1 teaspoon dried thyme

1 teaspoon baking soda (optional)

If using dried black-eyed peas, in a large saucepan, add 4 cups of water and the beans. Bring to a boil over high heat, then reduce the heat to low and simmer until the beans are soft, about 20 minutes. Turn off the heat, then drain and return the cooked peas to the saucepan. (If using canned beans, omit these steps and add the beans directly to the saucepan.)

Add the rice, 2 more cups of water, the coconut milk, onion, dried untoasted coconut, oil, salt, thyme, and baking soda (if using). Using a wooden spoon, stir gently to combine, and bring to a boil over high heat. Reduce the heat to low, cover the pot with a lid, and simmer, undisturbed, until the liquid is absorbed and the rice is tender, 30 to 40 minutes. Taste and adjust the seasoning with more salt as needed. Sprinkle with the toasted coconut and serve immediately.

THE INFAMOUS JOLLOF RICE!

SERVES 4 TO 6 AS A SIDE DISH ♉♉♉♉

In West Africa, one of the best-known nonviolent conflicts is the jollof wars. For decades, various representatives of West African countries have argued over who makes the best jollof rice. Ghanaians will swear theirs is clearly superior to the Nigerians'. Nigerians would die on their swords defending their recipe over any other—including that of the Senegalese, the originators of this deliciously controversial dish. We're almost as competitive about our jollof rice as we are about our soccer teams! Every person's jollof rice is slightly different, but there are regional identifiers, too. Senegalese jollof has lots of umami from fermented conch or fish; the Nigerian rendition is cooked almost to a burning point, giving it a unique smoky aroma; and the Ghanaians use curry powder, which makes theirs spicier. Because I'm Senegalese, I feel confident that ours is the clear winner. However, I am a peaceful person at heart, so I am perfectly happy to share the honor of having the best jollof rice with everybody else.

Jollof rice is one of the most universally loved grain dishes across West Africa, regardless of where your allegiances may lie. If you go to any West African buffet, or wedding, or festivity of any sort, you're sure to encounter this delicious tomato and rice dish next to a smorgasbord of other delightful foods like Roasted Piri-Piri Chicken (page 124), Poached Calamari Caldou in Tomato and Lemon Broth (page 150), and Spinach and Mushroom Efo Riro (page 182). Now, your home, too, can be one of the myriad places in the diaspora where this unifying dish is enjoyed.

My previous cookbooks had jollof rice recipes as part of other, more complex dishes, like deep-fried rice croquettes and thieboudienne (Senegal's national dish), but here I share a simple version that I kept vegan so that you can use it to accompany any meat or vegetable of your choice. I also use a two-step technique that's typical in Senegal for cooking the rice. It consists of first steaming the rice in a steamer, a couscoussier (see page 25), or a microwave, before finishing it in the tomato broth (see page 220 for details).

(RECIPE CONTINUES)

2 cups jasmine rice

¼ cup peanut or vegetable oil

1 cup chopped yellow onion

1 cup chopped green bell pepper

2 tablespoons tomato paste

1 cup peeled and chopped tomatoes or canned diced tomatoes with juice

3 cups vegetable stock or water

1 bay leaf

2 teaspoons fine sea salt

1½ teaspoons freshly ground black pepper

1 Scotch bonnet or habanero chili, left whole

THE TWO-STEP RICE METHOD

If you were to watch someone making jollof rice in Senegal, chances are you would see them steaming the rice over water in a couscoussier (see page 25). A couscoussier is a steamer of sorts, a cooking implement that looks like a pot with a perforated bottom nested inside another. If you don't have a couscoussier, you can use a regular steamer insert inside a larger pot with a lid. Or, if you don't have a steamer insert, you can put washed rice, just wet from rinsing in a microwave-safe bowl and cook for about 7 minutes. Stir and return the rice to the microwave for another 3 minutes to get to a similar partially cooked state.

The Senegalese use the two-step method to cook the rice until halfway done before allowing the rice to finish cooking in a sauce. This two-step method might seem cumbersome, but it's a great way to control the consistency of the rice and to prevent it from overcooking. To do this precooking the right way, put just enough water in the bottom pot so that it's a few inches deep but not touching the second pot. Rinse the rice with water several times, drain, and put it in the steamer insert, which goes in the larger pot. Then put the larger pot on the stove, cover it tightly with a lid, and bring the water to a boil over high heat. Lower the heat to medium and allow the gently boiling water to steam the rice until the rice is slightly translucent. Once the rice is half cooked, remove it from the heat and then proceed with your jollof making!

Rinse the rice several times until the water runs clear. Drain and set aside.

In a large pot, heat the oil over medium-high heat. When the oil begins to shimmer, add the onion and bell pepper. Cook, stirring with a wooden spoon, until they begin to soften, 3 minutes. Add the tomato paste and lower the heat to its lowest setting. Continue cooking, stirring often with a wooden spoon to avoid scorching, until the tomato paste begins to darken, 5 to 7 more minutes. Add the tomatoes and their juice and stir well to combine. Add the vegetable stock, bay leaf, salt, pepper, and Scotch bonnet. Increase the heat to high and bring to a boil. Reduce the heat to low and simmer until the oil begins to rise to the surface, 10 to 15 minutes. Remove the Scotch bonnet and set it aside.

Meanwhile, in a steamer or couscoussier, add the uncooked rice, cover tightly, and steam for about 15 minutes. You'll want to stir the rice once or twice to make sure it cooks evenly. (The rice is done when it is half cooked; the outer rim of each grain is translucent but it's still crunchy to the taste.) Remove and stir to prevent clumping.

Transfer the rice to the tomato broth. Stir and cover with a tight-fitting lid. Reduce the heat to the lowest setting and cook until the grains are soft, about 30 minutes. Uncover and stir to release the steam and fluff the grains. Taste to see that the grains are cooked. If not, add a few drops of water, cover again, and continue cooking for a few more minutes. Transfer to a platter and serve. Top with the Scotch bonnet for an added kick of spice.

NAIA'S JAZZY MAC AND CHEESE

SERVES 4 ♈♈♈♈

I love jazz music. Nothing gets me going like the bouncy riffs of my late friend and legendary pianist Randy Weston playing "Hi-Fly" on his baby grand piano, or the sultry, persuasive call and response between the trumpet and saxophone in "So What" by John Coltrane and Miles Davis. When captive Africans arrived on the shores of North America, they brought the musical and culinary rhythms of our motherland together with the resources available to them, eventually creating iconic contributions to music, dance, and food. Randy often said that jazz music should not be disassociated from its African roots. I feel the same way about food from our diaspora. Mac and cheese is a classic dish that represents the African diaspora in America and beyond, and I'm including it here as a reminder of its heritage. Thomas Jefferson is often credited with bringing mac and cheese to the United States, but it was James Hemings, his enslaved chef, who had trained in French cuisine and then introduced this dish to the White House and to his Black American community. I named this recipe after my daughter, Naia, because she loves mac and cheese, and because, when she's feeling extra jazzy, she hammers away on Lisa's piano like Thelonious Monk.

8 tablespoons (1 stick) unsalted butter, plus more for the pan

2 tablespoons kosher salt, for pasta water

1 pound elbow pasta

Extra-virgin olive oil, for tossing

4 cups grated medium-sharp Cheddar cheese

1 cup grated Gruyère cheese

1 cup shredded mozzarella cheese

½ cup all-purpose flour

2½ cups half-and-half

1½ cups whole milk

1½ teaspoons fine sea salt

½ teaspoon freshly ground black pepper

¼ teaspoon smoked paprika

Preheat the oven to 375°F. Grease a 9 × 13-inch broiler-proof dish with butter and set aside.

Bring a large pot of water to a boil over high heat and add the kosher salt. Add the pasta and cook according to the package directions until just shy of al dente. (Do not overcook the pasta.) Drain, transfer to a large bowl, and toss the pasta with a little bit of oil to keep it from sticking.

While the pasta is cooking, in a large bowl, toss the Cheddar, Gruyère, and mozzarella cheeses together to combine. Set aside.

In a large saucepan, melt the butter over low heat. Sprinkle in the flour and whisk to combine. Cook, whisking constantly, until thick and bubbly, about 2 minutes. In a medium bowl, combine the half-and-half and milk. Raise the heat under the saucepan slightly to medium and slowly pour in the milk mixture while whisking constantly. Reduce the heat to low and simmer the mixture until smooth and thick (similar to the consistency of condensed milk), about 10 minutes. Remove the pan from the heat and stir in the sea salt, pepper, and paprika, then gradually add 3 cups of the cheeses, stirring until completely melted and smooth.

Add the pasta to the saucepan of cheese sauce and stir to combine, then pour half of the pasta mixture into the prepared baking dish. Layer with 1½ cups of the remaining cheeses, then layer on the remaining pasta mixture. Sprinkle the top with the last 1½ cups of cheeses.

Bake until the cheeses are bubbly and lightly golden brown, about 30 minutes. (For a crispier top, place under the broiler for the last 3 minutes of cooking.) Serve immediately.

NORTHERN CALIFORNIA LIVING

California has the ideal climate for raising pretty much anything, from cows and goats to small children to your very own vegetable garden. The light is more beautiful, the sun brighter, the air fresher (at least it was, before wildfires became a seasonal occurrence). Drive several miles outside of any major city and you see rows and rows of avocado trees, lemon trees, big leafy greens, almonds, wine, olive oil . . . all things that are easy to love.

When Lisa suggested we move back to Northern California (her home for fifteen years before she moved to New York City), I had questions about what this would look like for me. Having spent so much of my life in bustling metropolises like Dakar and New York, I couldn't fully grasp what it meant to live in a slower-paced, more even-keeled environment. I also had really practical questions like, What if I feel the sudden urge to eat an oversize slice of cheese pizza at 11 p.m.? And would I really need to drive to a grocery store if I'm missing an ingredient for making dinner? But it was March 2020, and Lisa was pregnant, and there was the pandemic, which was rapidly and mercilessly amplifying the frequency of sirens outside of our Hell's Kitchen loft. We spent two weekends stuffing our belongings into large boxes, booked our flights, and made our escape from New York on a blustery afternoon, with our dog, Malcolm, Lisa's pregnant belly, and a pocket full of alcohol wipes. I remember how deserted Newark Liberty airport was, and how uncertain the future felt. Little did I know that at the other end of that transcontinental flight were treasures I would have never imagined in my wildest dreams.

A couple weeks later, Lisa chanced across a rental listing for a house in the East Bay hills outside San Francisco that didn't look very promising from either

the description or the photos. But we went to see it anyway, and as soon as we opened the front door, we found ourselves inside a magical midcentury home with sunlight streaming through panels of floor-to-ceiling windows, luminescent afternoon rays reflecting off the distant ocean waves under the Golden Gate Bridge. The backyard, which was dated and not very well kept, had four giant redwood trees and lots of overgrown herb bushes desperate for some water and a good trim. We instantly felt connected to the property and decided to make it our home. As we drove up to the neighborhood on the day we moved in, a couple baby deer gazed at us from behind some eucalyptus trees. It seemed as if every property on the street were a sanctuary for one delicious fruit after another: A fig tree with branches as robust as a baobab. An abundant Meyer lemon tree the size of an adult elephant. A jasmine trellis that infused an entire property wall with the scent of the most fragrant afternoon tea. A wild blackberry bush with vines that dip into a creek that serves as a watering hole for the coyotes that roam the hills. I had to do a double take. I was like, Wait, did I die and go to heaven? This place is incredible.

And then, of course, there was the arrival of Naia a few months later. She was born late at night via an unplanned C-section. After the doctors pulled her out, they handed her to nurses, who immediately took the screaming little bundle to a corner table to clean her up. Instinctively, I followed her there. I put out my hands and spoke to her gently, welcoming her into this world. Suddenly, the tiny child stopped crying. She

recognized my voice! This less-than-two-minute-old gift gripped my finger and squinted her not-yet-open eyes and—I swear—she smiled at me. A nurse snapped a photograph to capture this moment, the moment my life changed forever.

Today, Naia and I have the most delicious, unbreakable father-daughter bond. One of the silver linings of the pandemic was that, because all travel was halted, so far Naia has gotten to grow up with both her parents at home all the time. We play, we dance, we celebrate joy every day. She is also my most loyal and attentive sous-chef; we have a ritual of waking up and cooking breakfast together—Naia strapped to my chest in a little baby carrier, her tiny fingers grabbing at every sweet potato, okra pod, and fonio grain within her reach.

WEST AFRICA MEETS JAPAN FONIO PORRIDGE

SERVES 4 ΛΛΛΛ

One of the greatest unanticipated benefits of marrying Lisa was my discovery of Japanese breakfast. When we visited Tokyo, every morning her parents would bring out steamed white rice, tiny plates full of salty and sour condiments, freshly grilled fish, and hot green tea. This quickly became my favorite breakfast in the world. Now in California, Lisa often prepares Japanese okayu porridge for breakfast using a similar set of ingredients. She simmers day-old rice in a dried sardine broth, adds wakame seaweed and slow-scrambled eggs, and then tops it off with condiments and fish similar to the ones we eat at her parents' house. Lisa's okayu reminds me of a porridge that my grandmother used to make in Casamance in the south of Senegal—sometimes with chili and smoked sardines (called kethiakh), other times using poached chicken in a ginger lemon broth. My spin on this breakfast porridge is so easy to make and still gives you all the joy of a Japanese okayu or a Casamance porridge. I use fonio (see page 31) as the base and include smoky mackerel for a West African touch. If you don't have mackerel or herring, smoked salmon fillet works well, too. Feel free to add your favorite condiments to make it your own.

1 cup fonio

1 teaspoon grated fresh ginger

1 cup coarsely chopped smoked mackerel, smoked herring (skin off and bones removed), or smoked salmon

FOR SERVING (OPTIONAL)

Chopped scallions

Toasted sesame seeds

Umeboshi (Japanese pickled plums)

Lemon wedges

Chili powder (such as togarashi)

In a medium pot, combine the fonio, 4 cups of water, and the ginger. Cover and bring to a boil over high heat. Reduce the heat to its lowest setting, stir with a spoon once to make sure that the fonio is not sticking to the bottom of the pot, then cover again and simmer until the water is absorbed, 5 to 7 minutes. Remove from the heat and keep the pot covered for 5 more minutes, then check the fonio. It should be very soft and have a porridgelike consistency. Stir in the smoked mackerel.

TO SERVE: Transfer to bowls and top with the accompaniments of your choice.

FUFU

SERVES 4 ᴀᴀᴀᴀ

Everybody loves a good dumpling, so much so that I believe it's very important for every home cook to have a repertoire of these universally beloved delicacies to choose from. Here, I give you fufu, the quintessential African rendition. Fufu is a spongy dough typically prepared by boiling starchy vegetables like yams, cassavas, and plantains. It can even be made with beans or grains, like fonio (see page 215) or rice.

When traveling across the African continent, you'll encounter different versions of fufu—from the bustling city markets of Abidjan in Côte d'Ivoire to beachside snack stalls in Togo. (Fufu goes by different names, depending on where you encounter it: pap in South Africa, tô in Mali, and ugali in Kenya or Uganda. This version uses both plantain and cassava, and is sometimes called foutou.) It's a popular staple in countries like Haiti, Jamaica, and Cuba, too.

A wonderful benefit of the African dumpling is that it is really good for you! Fufu is rich in fiber and potassium, which help your gut regulate itself. Try serving it with Red Red Red (page 217), Seafood Okra Soupou Kanja (page 137), or Pumpkin Seed "Egusi" Stew with Eggplant and Collard Greens (page 180). Or, mix and match with pretty much anything for a creative twist to your serving of starch.

1 pound peeled fresh or frozen cassava
1 pound firm yellow plantains

If using fresh cassava, cut the cassava in half lengthwise to remove and discard the hard, fibrous core as needed (younger cassava don't have the fibrous core). Cut the fresh or frozen cassava into 2-inch cubes. In a medium bowl, soak the cubes in water to cover for about 15 minutes, then drain.

Peel the plantains and cut into 2-inch cubes.

Transfer the cassava and plantains to a blender or food processor and pour in ½ cup of water. Blend on medium power until smooth. Transfer the mixture to a large pot over medium-low heat. Cook, stirring frequently, until a thick paste forms, about 10 minutes. Add more water (about ½ cup) and cook, stirring often with a wooden spoon, until the dough becomes sticky and slightly springy, another 10 minutes.

Once the dough is cool enough to handle, divide the fufu into 8 individual portions, each slightly larger than a tennis ball. Using your hands, shape each portion into a ball. Serve immediately or wrap the balls individually in plastic wrap until ready to serve.

Fufu can be kept refrigerated tightly wrapped in plastic wrap for up to 5 days. Before eating, allow the dumplings to come to room temperature, or place them, unwrapped, in a bowl with a little sprinkle of water, and gently reheat in the microwave for 2 to 3 minutes.

CHICKPEA AND BELL PEPPER MOI MOI

SERVES 4 AS A SIDE DISH 𝄐𝄐𝄐𝄐

Moi moi rhymes with *joy,* and I like to believe that this is no accident. Moi moi is a joyful, healthy dish traditionally prepared by combining peeled black-eyed peas with seasoning and then wrapping and steaming the mixture in banana leaves. In this recipe, I use chickpeas instead of black-eyed peas and simply steam it in a cake pan. It comes out beautifully and can be used as a centerpiece on a vegetarian table. Moi moi is also a great baby food because it's soft, healthy, and portable! I love serving my moi moi with moyo sauce and The Infamous Jollof Rice! (page 219).

Moi moi keeps well in the freezer, so if you want to double the recipe, you're in luck.

1 cup dried chickpeas

1 cup chopped yellow onion

2 tablespoons vegetable oil, for the pan

2 tablespoons sustainably sourced red palm oil (see page 31) or vegetable oil

2 red bell peppers, finely chopped

1 habanero or Scotch bonnet chili, seeded and finely chopped (optional)

2 tablespoons ground dried crayfish (see page 34) or 2 tablespoons fish sauce (optional)

1 tablespoon fine sea salt

Hot water, as needed, for the pan

2 cups Moyo Sauce Goes with Everything (page 56), for serving

In a medium bowl, soak the chickpeas overnight in enough water to cover.

The next morning, drain the chickpeas. In a blender or food processor, add the onion and about ¼ cup of water and blend until smooth. Add the chickpeas and continue to blend on medium-high speed, occasionally stopping the motor to stir the mixture with a spoon to redistribute it. Repeat this process until the mixture has turned to a smooth paste (it should have the consistency of a thin batter, not too dense and not runny). Pour the chickpea mixture into a large bowl and set aside.

Place an oven rack in the middle of the oven. Preheat the oven to 350°F. Lightly grease a 9-inch round cake pan with the vegetable oil and place it inside a large baking pan.

In a large heavy-bottomed skillet, heat the red palm oil over medium-high heat. Add the bell peppers, habanero (if using), and ground crayfish (if using), and sauté until the bell peppers are soft, 3 to 5 minutes. Add the bell pepper mixture to the chickpea batter, season with the salt, and mix well to combine.

Spoon the batter into the cake pan until it reaches about two-thirds up the sides of the pan. Pour hot water into the baking pan until an inch or so of the cake pan sides are immersed in water. Cover the entire baking pan with aluminum foil and bake until a toothpick comes out clean when inserted into the middle of the pudding, about 1 hour. Remove the pan from the oven and let it rest at room temperature, covered and still sitting in the hot water bath, for about 10 minutes. Carefully remove the cake pan from the hot water bath and, using a kitchen towel or mitten so you don't burn yourself, invert the pudding onto a serving plate or platter. Serve with the moyo sauce. To freeze, allow the moi moi to cool to room temperature, then wrap it in aluminum foil and store for up to a month.

ACKNOWLEDGMENTS

We love our family as much as we love food.

THANK YOU FOR YOUR ENDLESS LOVE AND SUPPORT, TO . . .

Our daughter, Naia

Her older siblings, Sitoë,
Elijah, and Haroun

Our dog, Malcolm

Our Senegalese family:
Aunt Marie, Uncle Joseph, Alain,
Jean-Louis, Gina, Kiki, Anatole,
Loulou, Touty, Papis, Néné, Patrice,
Miki, Amsy, Anne Cécile,
and Yvonne

Our family in Japan,
Hawaii, and California:
Mary, Sho, Yushi, Shota,
Masa-san, Annie, Rick, Joy,
Grey, Aunt Ji Li

Our amazing friends, neighbors,
and collaborators from
all over the world

THOSE WITHOUT WHOM THIS BOOK COULD NOT HAVE BEEN CREATED:

Evan Sung, for the beautiful photos

Leila Nichols, for the lovely prop styling

Violeta Callejas, for being Naia's nanny and
Pierre's right hand in the kitchen

Amethyst Ganaway, for testing the recipes

Rush Jackson, for designing
the cover and pages

The Clarkson Potter team: Jennifer Sit,
Marysarah Quinn, Terry Deal,
Natalie Blachere, Phil Leung,
Monica Stanton, and Kristin Casemore

Our agent Kitty Cowles

LAST, BUT NOT LEAST, WE WOULD LIKE TO THANK EACH OTHER:

Lisa was in the conversations from the beginning, and it felt only natural that she would come on this journey.

This book has been a true partnership between Pierre's story and recipes, and Lisa's deep understanding of Pierre and of the written word.

THANK YOU, PIERRE—

For having a story worth telling.

THANK YOU, LISA—

For finding the words to tell it with.

INDEX

Note: Page references in *italics* indicate photographs. Page references in **bold** indicate where recipe is used as an ingredient or accompaniment.